HOSEA: PROPHET OF GOD'S LOVE

A Study Guide and Exposition of the Book of Hosea

T. Miles Bennett

BAKER BOOK HOUSE
Grand Rapids, Michigan

*To the STUDENTS
who have shared with me in
the DISCOVERY of the
priceless TREASURES
of the
PROPHETS*

ISBN: 0-8010-0645-7
©1975 by Baker Book House Company
Printed in the United States of America

CONTENTS

Continued

PREFACE

Who can plumb the depths of God's nature? Who can comprehend the multitudinous rays of His attributes shining forth from the very essence of His Being? No one, of course. But God in His concern for man gave through man partial revelations of Himself, against that time when He was fully revealed in His Son, Jesus Christ.

The prophet Hosea was uniquely used of God to make a significant contribution to the fuller understanding of the nature of God. By the prophet's day God's power, wrath, and justice were widely recognized and accepted. This very fact made more difficult man's acceptance of His love. It remained, then, for Hosea to magnify the divine love, and he did it in such marvelous fashion that in time love became as much an attribute of Divinity as the justice proclaimed by Amos (a near contemporary of Hosea). In fact it was Hosea who learned first that the essence of the divine nature was not justice but love. It was he who left this sublime truth as a legacy which is the only basis of hope for any man. God grant that your study of the prophet's message will give you a clearer vision of the undying love of God for man, and inspire you to share it with a love-starved world.

T. Miles Bennett
Southwestern Seminary
Fort Worth, Texas

OUTLINE OF
THE BOOK OF HOSEA

PART ONE / GOD'S WORD THROUGH HOSEA'S
MARRIAGE: Revelation in Heartache
(1:1–3:5)

Title Verse (1:1)

A. HOSEA'S MARRIAGE AND CHILDREN (1:2-9)
1. His Marriage to Gomer (1:2-3a)
2. The Birth of Three Children (1:3b-9)

B. RESTORATION OF ISRAEL AND JUDAH
(1:10-11)

C. GOMER'S UNFAITHFULNESS TO HOSEA
SYMBOLICAL OF ISRAEL'S INFIDELITY TO
YAHWEH: WORDS OF JUDGMENT (2:1-23)
1. The Faithlessness of Israel (2:2-5)
2. The Consequences of Israel's Infidelity
(2:6-13)
   a. Frustration and despair (2:6-8)
   b. The penalty of privation (2:9-13)
3. The Goal of Judgment: Renewal and Re-
betrothal (2:14-23)

D. HOSEA'S LOVE FOR GOMER ILLUSTRATIVE
OF GOD'S LOVE FOR ISRAEL (3:1-5)
1. Hosea Redeems His Unfaithful Wife (3:1-3)
2. The Message for Israel (3:4-5)

INTRODUCTION

The Minor Prophets

In the Hebrew Canon the prophets from Hosea to Malachi form a single book called "The Twelve." The designation "Minor Prophets" as compared to the "Major Prophets" was first given to them by Augustine (*City of God,* 18:29). The "Minor Prophets" are so named because of their length, not because they are of lesser importance. They are minor in volume but not in value. Ancient Jewish interpreters held that the Book of Hosea was placed first because of the interpretation put upon "when the Lord *first* spoke through Hosea" (1:2). More recent scholars, and correctly so, hold that Hosea stands first not in order of time, but because of its length and the richness of its content.

The Prophet Hosea

Hosea alone of all the prophets was a native of the northern kingdom of Israel, to which only he and Amos prophesied. The prophet's name is identical with that of Joshua ("Yahweh delivers") in its original form (Num. 13:8) and Hoshea, the last king of Israel (2 Kings 15:30). It is significant to note that the name *Jesus* is the Greek form of the word whose root meaning is "space" or "room," hence "deliverance" or "salvation." The words of the angel to Joseph come to mind, "You shall call his name Jesus, for he will save his people from their sins" (Matt. 1:21).

The only source of information concerning Hosea is the book which bears his name, and surprisingly few details are given there. The major fact told about his life is that he married Gomer the daughter of Diblaim who became unfaithful to him perhaps after the birth of their three children. Sometime after Hosea had driven her from his home or after she had left of her own accord, the prophet bought her from slavery, and sought to reform her by a temporary confinement. Whether Diblaim is her father's name or the name of her birthplace remains uncertain. There is greater certainty concerning the name of Hosea's father (Beeri, 1:1), though little or nothing is known concerning him.

Numerous surmises (guesses?) have been made as to Hosea's occupation prior to his becoming a prophet. Pointing to his seeming knowledge of the work of the priests, both as the official representatives of the cult and as judges and teachers (4:6-8; 5:1; 6:9), some have concluded that Hosea was professionally connected with them. Others, arguing from the presence of numerous illustrations from agricultural life, have asserted that he was a farmer. And still others have conjectured that he was a baker, or at least must have lived near a public bakery, for he draws illustrations from the fiery oven (see 7:4-8). It seems the part of wisdom to leave the question of his occupation unanswered.

The superscription, or title verse (1:1), places Hosea's ministry in the reign of Jeroboam II, king of Israel, and in the reigns of Uzziah, Jotham, Ahaz, and Hezekiah, kings of Judah. There is no problem relative to Hosea's ministry beginning prior to the death of Jeroboam II (ca. 750 B.C.). Some difficulty arises, however, with extending his ministry into the time of Hezekiah, king of Judah, who began his reign no earlier than 715-16 B.C. There is no evidence in the Book of Hosea that the prophet's ministry included the fall of the kingdom of Israel to the Assyrians in 721-22 B.C. Nevertheless the information contained in the verse is trustworthy in its indication that Hosea's ministry continued beyond the reign of Jeroboam II into the chaotic period of the six kings who succeeded him before the nation's fall. But just how far into this period of confusion and anarchy Hosea's ministry extended, it is difficult to determine—perhaps no later than 735 B.C. While the actual length of his ministry may have to remain in doubt, it is rather certain that the early years of that ministry were contemporary with the prophet Amos, also of the northern kingdom, and in its later years contemporary with Isaiah and Micah, prophets of the kingdom of Judah.

Little is known about the final years of Hosea's life. A Jewish legend states that the prophet died in Babylon and that his body was brought back to Palestine and buried at Safed, northwest of the Sea of Galilee. According to a second tradition he was a native of Gilead and was buried there. Today the grave of Nebi Osha may be seen near es-Salt, Ramoth-Gilead, south of the Jabbok River.[1]

The Book of Hosea

The material in Hosea is unique among the Prophetic Books in its division into two distinct but unequal parts. The first part (chaps. 1–3), which may be regarded as introductory to the remaining material, deals with the marriage of Hosea and its meaning for Israel's relations

1. Fredrick C. Eiselen, *The Prophetic Books of the Old Testament* (New York: The Methodist Book Concern, 1923), p. 372.

with Yahweh. The second division (chaps. 4–14), sometimes called the "Second Book of Hosea," is lacking in a central, unifying theme around which the materials may be logically arranged. Rather, it is composed of a number of independent discourses, with no sharp line of separation between them. Consequently any analysis of the text is more or less arbitrary.

It has been conjectured that the materials in the two-fold division of the book circulated originally as two independent manuscripts, the first under the title, *Autobiographical Reflections of Hosea* and the second, *Prophecies of Hosea*. Which of the two sections originated first cannot be known with certainty. It is highly probable, however, that the autobiographical material (1–3) was composed toward the close of the prophet's life and that at least portions of the remaining chapters (4–14) must have originated earlier.

It has also been conjectured, largely due to stylistic differences, that the two divisions are from different hands. G. A. Smith has pointed to one scholar who distinguishes two Hoseas separated by a period of some fifty years.[2] Smith disagrees and correctly holds that the altered outlook of the second section from that of the first results from changed political conditions, and that the difference in style is due to a difference of occasion and motive. He points out, and rightly so, that the two divisions contain identical religious principles as well as numerous characteristic expressions, and that "there breathes throughout the two sections the same urgent and jealous temper, which renders Hosea's personality distinctive among the prophets."[3]

The Book of Hosea is difficult to read and its mean-

---

2. George Adam Smith, *The Book of the Twelve Prophets*, vol. 1 (New York: Harper & Brothers, 1928), p. 219.

3. Ibid., p. 220.

ing is obscure in numerous places. This is due first of all to its style, which differs radically from that of any other of the prophetical writings. Jerome described it as "consisting of short clauses." Another wrote, "Each verse forms a whole by itself, like one heavy toll in a funeral knell." Still another has added, "Even the fetters of grammar are almost too much for Hosea's vehement feeling." And herein lies a major cause of the abrupt and disconnected nature of so much of the Book of Hosea, especially chapters 4–14. Hosea was a man of very sensitive nature. His emotions were easily stirred. And stirred they were by the unfaithful conduct of his wife, whom he deeply loved, and by the "whoredoms" of his nation, also dearly beloved by the prophet.

As a result his writings are highly surcharged with feeling and have been fittingly described as "a succession of sobs." Consequently he could not deliver a stately and connected discourse. The truth burned in his heart. In sympathy and anguish he poured out that heart without attempting to indicate the logical connection between his separate utterances. Hosea was a man of moods, and these moods found expression in his messages. Hence he did not so much address an audience as commune with himself "in shuddering disjointed monologue." Little wonder, then, that order and sequence are almost totally lacking in his messages.

A second problem in connection with the Book of Hosea relates to the text, described by one Old Testament scholar as "one of the most dilapidated in the Old Testament, and in parts beyond repair."[4] The Hebrew text of Hosea is difficult to translate at a number of points and almost without meaning unless use is made of other ancient versions, e.g., the Septuagint (Greek version of the Old Testament). The reader has only to ob-

---

4. Ibid., p. 228.

serve the many marginal notes in the Revised Standard Version in order to see the difficulties of translating this prophetic book. Such difficulties are due first of all to poor compilation and transmission of the prophet's messages, but also to the prophet's unique style. His emotional and highly sensitive nature is reflected in short, broken sentences, frequently lacking in either logical or syntactical connection. Hence it is difficult to decide when his words have been lost as the result of textual confusion and when they are before us in the exact order of the prophet's disordered emotions. In any case, and in this we are most fortunate, it is not hard to discover the fundamental message of this prophet—the undying love of God for man (Israel).

A third difficulty of the Book of Hosea relates to the prophet's marriage, specifically to the interpretation of chapter 1, verses 2 and 3: "When the Lord first spoke through Hosea, the Lord said to Hosea, 'Go, take to yourself a wife of harlotry and have children of harlotry. . . .' So he went and took Gomer the daughter of Diblaim. . . ." Various interpretations of these verses have been given, broadly categorized as follows: (1) allegorical, which holds that Hosea never actually married and that the account is an allegory, not real history; (2) those interpretations which propose that Hosea did actually marry, but disagree as to whether the bride was or was not an adulteress at the time of the marriage.

The allegorical approach has proved popular with those who have felt compelled to find a way out of the moral difficulty in the marriage of one of God's spokesmen to a "woman of the street."[5] However, a number of arguments weigh rather heavily against the symbolical or nonhistorical interpretation: First, the style is clearly

---

5. Edward J. Young, *Introduction to the Old Testament* (Grand Rapids: Eerdmans Publishing Co., 1949), pp. 245f.

that of a narrative rather than a parable or an allegory. Simple facts are told—for example, the weaning of the child (1:8)—and there is no effort to make the details symbolic, except as indicated in the naming of the children. The names Gomer and Diblaim belong to real people, and all attempts to find symbolic value in them have failed. Second, such an interpretation does not remove the moral difficulty, since it is just as derogatory to God and one of His prophets to ascribe such action to them in parable as in actual fact. Furthermore, if Hosea had a faithful wife, it seems incredible that he would have exposed her to a suspicion of infidelity and unchastity as such allegorical usage would have done.

A larger number of interpreters, ancient and modern, presuppose the historicity of the marriage narrative and take the story as the literal account of actual facts. The proponents of this view fall into two basic groups: (1) those who hold that Gomer was a harlot, either profane or sacred,[6] and that Hosea's marriage to her was a symbolic act witnessing to God's love for unfaithful Israel;[7] and, (2) those who insist that Gomer was not a harlot at the time of marriage, but a woman of unchaste disposition. Evil tendencies were within her, but they were yet to manifest themselves. Finally they became so strong that Gomer deserted the prophet either for her lovers or for the licentious rites connected with the worship of Baal.[8]

In regard to the view which holds that Gomer was a harlot at the time of her marriage to Hosea, there are

6. Roy L. Honeycutt, "Hosea," *Broadman Bible Commentary,* vol. 7 (Nashville: Broadman Press, 1972), pp. 3f.

7. See J. Powis Smith, *The Prophet and His Problems* (New York: Charles Scribner's Sons, 1914), pp. 109-23.

8. See George Adam Smith, *Twelve Prophets,* pp. 246-52.

19

two objections which render this approach invalid. In the first place, such an interpretation does not suit or correspond to the symbolism involved. The relation between Hosea and Gomer is symbolical of the relation between Yahweh and Israel. Hosea, and others of the early prophets, looked upon Israel as pure at the beginning of the union with Yahweh, only corrupting herself at some later time. In order, then, to have consistent symbolism, Gomer must have been pure when Hosea married her, becoming corrupt only at a later date. In the second place, a question may be raised as to how a wise and holy God could have given such a command to one of His servants.[9] An alliance of this character would have exposed the prophet inevitably to contempt, leaving the impression that he was condoning the conduct of his countrymen, when his mission was, rather, to condemn it.

One is left, then, with the only interpretation consistent with the character of God, the character and teaching of Hosea, and at the same time true to the analogy he draws between his own experience with Gomer and Yahweh's experience with Israel. Gomer was not a harlot at the time of her marriage and remained unstained until sometime after the birth of her first child, if not until after the birth of all three children. She is called "a wife of harlotry" (1:2) not because she was already such, but because she later proved to be such a person. Evil tendencies were dormant in her heart, and the prophet's love was not adequate to restrain them. His love aroused no permanent response in her heart, so she left him for the wild orgies of the sensuous worship of Baal. As Hosea brooded over the tragedy of his own household, he was divinely enabled to see in it a reflection of Yahweh's experience with Israel, of God's love for His peo-

9. See K. Owen White, *Studies in Hosea* (Nashville: Convention Press, 1957), pp. 17ff.

20

ple and of their ingratitude and lack of loyalty to Him. Hosea was already familiar with the unfaithfulness and moral degradation of Israel and had sought to express some of the possible consequences of it in the symbolic names of his children (1:4-9), but when the truth about Gomer became known, the conviction grew within him that his marriage was neither an accident nor pure misfortune. Rather, it was God's way of speaking to him concerning His wayward people. In other words, Hosea's account of his marriage was colored by his feelings as he looked back upon the event. It was only upon reflection, after he had learned of Gomer's true character and after he had seen in her desertion a symbol of Israel's apostasy from God, that it could be said of Hosea that when the Lord first spoke through him, he said, "Go, take to yourself a wife of harlotry" (1:2a).[10]

The uniqueness of Hosea's message lies in the fact that he learned it out of his own personal sufferings. The experience of his wife's unfaithfulness and his heartrending attempts to woo her back were the means God used to reveal to the prophet that Israel's lack of faithfulness was being met by just such a love from the very God whose covenant she had so flagrantly violated. So this message was concerned with the steadfastness of God's love and the persistent unfaithfulness of Israel. These two themes with variations appear throughout his book and are crystallized in God's requirements of Israel, stated in 6:6.

---

10. A related problem is the relationship of the woman of chapter 3 to Gomer of chapter 1 (see pp. 43-44).

QUESTIONS FOR DISCUSSION

1. Distinguish between the "Major Prophets" and the "Minor Prophets" of the Old Testa-

ment. Is the distinction made on the basis of their comparative significance? Name four prophets belonging to each group.

2. What is *your* definition of a prophet? Does it include the idea that he was a *man*? that he spoke to *men*? that his message was from *God*?

3. Is it correct to look upon the prophets as "divine dictaphones," uttering truths about which they understood little or nothing? Does the fact that a prophet was inspired by God imply that he no longer had any human limitations?

4. What are some of the basic facts known about the prophet Hosea? Is he referred to elsewhere in the Old Testament? Are other prophets of the Old Testament referred to by other writers of the Old Testament? Cite any examples with which you are familiar.

5. What evidence can you cite from the Book of Hosea that the prophet was a farmer? a priest? a baker?

6. What are three major problems that confront one in the study of the Book of Hosea?

Influence of Hosea and His Message

We know very little of the effect which Hosea's message produced on his hearers, except that there is a hint of persecution in one of the chapters (9:7ff.). But that there were some who were moved by his words is evidenced by the very fact that they were collected and preserved for future generations. Further evidence of the influence of Hosea and his teachings is found in the material belonging to later prophets. One finds his influence, for example, in Isaiah's attitude toward the system of worship ritual (Isa. 1:10-17) and in his opposition to foreign alliances (see, e.g., Isa. 36:6). Hosea's symbolic use of the marriage relationship to portray Israel's relation to Yahweh reappears in Ezekiel, where Jerusalem's idolatry is denounced as adultery and fornication (Ezek. 16; 23).

It was on a prophet of the following century, Jeremiah of Anathoth, that Hosea's influence was most keenly felt. He found in Hosea not only a teacher, but a spirit akin to his own. Both were men of unusually emotional and tender temperaments, overwhelmed with compassion for the very people whose judgments they were compelled to announce. They have been correctly described as "the two martyr prophets of the Old Testament, men of sorrows and acquainted with grief." The younger prophet was indebted to the older for numerous ideas and for the imagery in which they were clothed, for example, his concept of Yahweh as the husband of Israel (Jer. 2:2), his characterization of idolatry as fornication and adultery (Jer. 7:9), and his idealization of the wilderness sojourn as the time when Israel's relation to Yahweh was perfect and complete (Jer. 2:2ff.). The influence Hosea exerted can be seen also in the book's use in the New Testament where more than thirty quotations, either direct or indirect, are found.[11]

Hosea's ministry, then, was certainly not in vain. The nation, it is true, was deaf to his appeals, and the exile became its grave. But his message was preserved and passed on, and succeeding generations have been blessed by it. Hosea was the first to interpret religion so absolutely in terms of love, a fact which prompted George

---

11. Hobart Freeman, *An Introduction to the Old Testament Prophets* (Chicago: Moody Press, 1968), p. 173.

Adam Smith to write, "There is no truth uttered by later prophets about the divine grace, which we do not find in germ in him. . . . He is the first prophet of grace, Israel's first evangelist."[12] Carl Cornill was more inclusive when he wrote, "When we consider that all this was . . . new, that those thoughts in which humanity has been educated and which have consoled it for nearly three thousand years, were first spoken by Hosea, we must reckon him among the greatest religious geniuses which the world has ever produced."[13] One might question the absolute newness of Hosea's doctrine of divine love, but that it was expressed with a finality and clarity unknown before his time is without question. Hosea was undoubtedly one of the greatest of the prophets. With Amos and Isaiah he laid the foundations of literary prophecy, and hence must be counted as one of the most important agents through whom God chose to reveal Himself to Israel.

The Times of the Prophet

The period of Hosea's prophetic ministry is twice defined (1:1). On the one hand it is described as occurring "in the days of Jeroboam the son of Joash, king of Israel," that is, during the time between 786-746 B.C. On the other hand the prophet's activity is located "in the days of Uzziah, Jotham, Ahaz, and Hezekiah, kings of Judah." By this latter statement the writer hardly meant to state that Hosea's prophetic activity spanned a period of approximately one hundred years (ca. 786-687 B.C.). It is more probable that he meant to suggest no more than that Hosea was a contemporary of Isaiah.

---

12. George Adam Smith, *Twelve Prophets*, p. 239.

13. Carl H. Cornill, *The Prophets of Israel* (Chicago: Open Court Publishing Co., 1897), p. 50.

This was accomplished by using the same kings of Judah to date Hosea as were used to date Isaiah (cf. Isa. 1:1). The writer, then, was not so much interested in establishing specific chronological limits for Hosea's ministry as he was in making clear that the prophet's ministry was associated with the final days of Jeroboam II and that he was a contemporary of Isaiah. Although the specific limits of Hosea's activity are difficult to establish, it seems certain that it began prior to the death of Jeroboam II (ca. 748 B.C.) and ended prior to the fall of Samaria, capital city of Israel, to the Assyrians in 722 B.C.

The historical record in II Kings 14—17 gives witness to the fact that Hosea exercised his ministry during perhaps the most chaotic period in the entire history of the northern kingdom of Israel—a period filled with strife, disorder, and bloodshed. Hosea began his ministry during the kingship of Jeroboam II. Israel was at the summit of military power and national prestige and at the same time far down the slope of a fatal moral decline. Jeroboam was the last strong man of Israel and following his death rival politicians were quick to sacrifice the nation's interests to their own selfish desires. Of the six kings who succeeded Jeroboam only one, or possibly two, experienced a natural death. In their desperation the kings looked first one way and then another to secure foreign help. Israel paid tribute first to Assyria, then to Egypt, until at last she lost her independence, exhausted her sources, and finally was forced to accept total subjection to Assyria. With her independence gone, Israel's decline was rapid. All classes of society became corrupt. Priests turned to robbery and rejoiced in the sin of the people inasmuch as it increased their own wealth. Conditions became so corrupt, Hosea cried out, "There is no faithfulness or kindness, and no knowledge of God in the land; there is swearing, lying, killing, stealing, and committing adultery . . . " (4:1-2). Religion became associated with the most sensuous and idolatrous practices.[14] The people confused the worship of Yahweh with Baal, and calf worship was a common occurrence. Family life especially became dissolute, and upon such loose living the prophet laid his heaviest indictment, describing it with the harsh word *whoredom* seventeen times. In brief, moral and spiritual decline, political chaos, idolatrous worship, and apostasy from Yahweh characterized the nation to whom Hosea was commissioned to announce words of rebuke, warning, judgment, and hope.

Hosea and Amos

A study of Hosea and his times would not be complete without giving some attention to a near, if not an actual, contemporary of his, the prophet Amos. In fact, a careful reading of the Book of Amos proves rewarding as a background to the messages of Hosea. Hosea presents a striking contrast to Amos and, in the end, supplements him. Amos thunders the harsh and unyielding justice and wrath of God; Hosea woos, exhorts, and pleads in the name of the steadfast love of God. Amos's harshest criticism is concerned with man's inhumanity to man, while Hosea is overwhelmed with man's disloyalty to God. Amos is awed by the thought of God's righteousness, while Hosea is subdued by the vision of His love. Amos has scarcely a word of hope for Israel; Hosea finds a moral basis for hope in the love of God and the repentance of the people. Amos spoke of Yahweh as the sovereign Lord of the universe, ruling and judging the nations as well as His own people. Hosea's message is limited to the chosen people. He is completely silent about the destiny of the nations.

---

14. Canaanite theology and religious practices are of extreme importance to an understanding of the Book of Hosea. See Roy L. Honeycutt, "Hosea," pp. 3ff.

The two prophets, then, supplement and complete each other. Justice is the underlying principle in regulating man's relationship to man. But justice alone is inadequate and must be supplemented with what Hosea called loving-kindness. The rabbinic sages were right when they brought Amos and Hosea together in one harmonious whole: "When the Creator, blessed be His name," they said, "saw that man could not endure if measured by the attributes of strict justice, He joined His attribute of mercy to that of justice, and created man by the combined principle of both."[15]

15. Beryl D. Cohon, *The Prophets* (New York: Bloch Publishing Co., 1960), p. 50.

QUESTIONS FOR DISCUSSION

1. Which Old Testament prophet did Hosea influence in a decisive manner? Give evidence of this influence by citing examples from Scripture.
2. Does the fact that the prophets spoke to men emphasize the principle that their messages were related to the historical situation of their hearers? Does this limit the possibility of predictive prophecy, since in such prophecy the prophet is not speaking to his day but to some future day?
3. Is it not true that the prophets spoke first of all to the people of their own day? Is it not necessary, then, to learn all one can about the historical situation out of which the prophet's message originated?
4. Will the reading of 2 Kings 14—15 and the Book of Amos add to one's knowledge of

the background of Hosea's day? Check these passages and point out what they reveal about the moral and spiritual conditions of his time.

5. Both Amos and Hosea were God's spokesmen to the northern kingdom of Israel. They were near contemporaries and Amos's ministry occurred first. Would not the study of the Book of Amos provide a rich background for the understanding of Hosea's messages? What is the major emphasis of each prophet? How account for such a sharp difference in emphasis? Would a difference in place of birth, occupation, and life experiences help to explain the difference?

Part One
GOD'S WORD THROUGH HOSEA'S MARRIAGE: REVELATION IN HEARTACHE
(Hosea 1:1 – 3:5)

God used the experiences of His people to reveal Himself in the Old Testament in preparation for the full revelation of Himself in His Son, Jesus Christ. This is particularly true in the case of Hosea. Possessed of a warm and affectionate nature and the God-given ability to forgive, he revealed much of the love and forgiving grace of God in a bitter experience in his own life—the unfaithfulness of his wife, Gomer. In this tragic domestic trial he learned much of the cruel wrong of Israel's unfaithfulness to Yahweh and of Yahweh's unquenchable love for Israel.

Title Verse (1:1). Hosea's prophecy begins with a significant statement, "The word of the Lord that came to Hosea" which may be translated, "The beginning of that which Jehovah spoke by Hosea." God was not only speaking to Hosea, but through him He was speaking to others. A fundamental tenet of Hebrew prophecy is the conviction that God's word comes to the prophet (cf. Mic. 1:1; Joel 1:1; Jer. 1:1). The prophet's inspiration was not of himself, but of God, who was willing to reveal Himself to His people through the prophet. This gave authority to the prophet's preaching and urgency to his demands.

Hosea was the son of Beeri of whom nothing is

known, but whose name means "my well." Early Jewish writers mistakenly identified him with Beerah (I Chron. 5:6), who was carried into captivity by Tiglath-pileser.

The period of Hosea's prophetic activity is doubly defined as "in the days of Jeroboam . . . the king of Israel" and "in the days of Uzziah, Jotham, Ahaz, and Hezekiah, kings of Judah." (See Introduction, pages 14-15; 24-25 for the difficulty involved in trying to reconcile these two periods.) There is evidence in the book that Hosea began his ministry in the reign of Jeroboam II (786-746 B.C.) but no evidence that it continued as late as the beginning of Hezekiah's reign (ca. 715 B.C.). The consensus of opinion relative to the time of Hosea's ministry seems to place it in the period 750-735 B.C.

A. Hosea's Marriage and Children (1:2-9)

1. His Marriage to Gomer (1:2-3a)

Hosea was told to marry "a wife of harlotry and have children of harlotry." Conflicting viewpoints have arisen relative to the interpretation of this command (see Introduction pp. 18-21). Do we have here only a parable or allegory? Or did a marriage actually take place? If so, was Gomer a harlot at the time of the marriage? This writer feels that these questions are best answered by the approach that a marriage actually took place but that Gomer was not guilty of adultery until sometime later, perhaps after the birth of all three children. Such a view is not only consistent with the character and nature of God but also with the symbolism involved in the account. The relation between Hosea and Gomer was symbolical of that between Yahweh and Israel. Hosea considered Israel as pure at the beginning of her relationship with Yahweh, corrupting herself only at some later time. For the symbolism to be consistent, then, Gomer would need to have been pure at the beginning of her marriage with Hosea. Otherwise the symbolism breaks down. Such an approach is further verified by the statement "for the land commits great harlotry by forsaking the Lord" (v. 2). "The land" stands for the people; "great harlotry" summarizes their unfaithfulness to Yahweh. In similar manner Gomer committed great harlotry in departing from Hosea. As Hosea's wife had proved untrue to him, so Israel was untrue to Yahweh.

"Gomer the daughter of Diblaim," was Hosea's wife. The name was a common one and there is no ground for reading into it an allegorical meaning. If the prophet had intended such, he would have indicated it just as he did in the case of his children (see next paragraph).

2. The Birth of Three Children (1:3b-9)

To Hosea and Gomer three children were born, and to each was given a prophetic name pointing to God's punishment of His people for their sins. The first child, a son, was called Jezreel meaning "God scatters" or "God sows." The name had a twofold significance: (1) After the people of Israel had been *scattered* because of their sins, God would *sow* or plant them in their own land again; and, (2) sins commited in the valley of Jezreel by Ahab would be punished, and there Israel would taste defeat. The name points both backward and forward— backward to the massacre of Ahab's family by Jehu (2 Kings 9–10), and forward to the punishment of that cruel act. Referring to His judgment God said, "I will break the bow of Israel." The bow stands for the might of Israel which was soon to be ended. A broken bow was a sign of impotence.

The second child, a girl, was named Lo-ruhamah, meaning "no pity," "no mercy," or "that hath not obtained mercy." The child's name was to indicate to the people of Israel that they could expect no mercy from God. As the "unpitied one" she symbolized the plight of the northern kingdom of Israel which had sinned against Yahweh and was ripe for judgment.

In contrast to Israel's imminent fall God would have mercy on the house of Judah to save it (1:7). However, the salvation would be of Yahweh and not by military might (see Isa. 37:36; 2 Kings 19:35).

The second son born to Hosea and Gomer bore the name Lo-ammi, meaning "not my people." God would no longer claim Israel as His own, nor be their God; they were to be rejected. At Sinai Israel had covenanted to be Yahweh's people and He to be their God (Exod. 19:1-8). They repeatedly broke that covenant, so Hosea declares that they will be rejected, a rejection which will result in the exile and destruction of the kingdom of Israel as a political entity.

It is noteworthy to observe the climax suggested by the three names: *Jezreel* announces God's judgment; *Lo-ruhamah*, the withdrawal of His compassion; and *Lo-ammi*, His treatment of Israel as a foreign people.

B. Restoration of Israel and Judah (1:10-11)

The finality of the messages of doom symbolized by the names of Hosea's children is tempered by the prospect of mercy for Judah (1:7), and the promised restoration of the united kingdoms (Israel and Judah) when Yahweh's covenant mercies will be renewed and the name *Jezreel*, which formerly symbolized judgment, will instead signify coming restoration and glory (1:11).

Here we find one of those swift transitions from judgment to mercy which are so characteristic of the prophets, especially of Hosea. He never pronounces doom upon his people but that he follows it with a declaration of God's mercy. Rather abruptly Hosea turns from tragedy to promise. He affirms that God's promise to Abraham (Gen. 22:17) will yet be fulfilled. Israel's posterity will be as numberless as the sand of the sea (1:10), and instead of bearing the name Lo-ammi, "Not my people," they shall be called "Sons of the living God." (See Paul's application of this passage in Romans 9:24-26.) Hosea did not completely erase the possibility of salvation previously promised by God. The final punishment predicted would yet be modified by the eternal "nevertheless" of promises previously made.

Judah and Israel are spoken of together (1:11) to indicate that God's plan for His chosen people was that they should be a united nation. Later prophets emphasized the same truth (cf. Jer. 3:18; 50:4-5; Ezek. 37:16-22). United under one head, "they shall go up from the land [that is, from the small land of Palestine they shall spread out far beyond it], for great shall be the day of Jezreel." It will be great because Yahweh will no longer *scatter* His people, but *sow* them and cause them to grow. In that day the name of Hosea's first son will no longer be baneful, but blessed; no longer the name for a day of judgment upon Israel, but a day of Yahweh's *sowing* from which will come a glorious increase. Neither will the names of Hosea's other children be appropriate as symbolical of Yahweh's relationship to His people. In the day God *sows* His people the gracious designations *Ammi* (My people) and *Ruhamah* (Pitied) will replace *Lo-ammi* (Not my people) and *Lo-ruhamah* (Not pitied) (2:1).[1]

---

1. The chapter division here is unfortunate since the thought of the first verse of chapter 2 concludes that of chapter 1.

QUESTIONS FOR DISCUSSION

1. Discuss several possible meanings or interpretations of God's instruction to Hosea in 1:2. With which do you agree? Why?

33

2. Is Hosea the only prophet to describe the relationship between Yahweh and His people as that of husband and wife (see Jer. 2:1-2)? Why use human analogies (comparisons) when speaking of God? Why not make use of a "divine" vocabulary?

3. In our day does an individual's name have any particular use or significance other than for the purpose of identification? Was this true in Hosea's time? What is the significance of the names of Hosea's three children?

4. Is it valid to assign Hosea's references to the southern kingdom of Judah (e.g., in 1:11) to a later writer (editor)? What was the attitude of other prophets toward the restoration of God's people to Palestine? Were both kingdoms (Israel and Judah) to be included? (See Jer. 30:1-11; Ezek. 37:15-23.)

C. Gomer's Unfaithfulness to Hosea Symbolical of Israel's Infidelity to Yahweh: Words of Judgment (2:1-23)

From his thoughts concerning Israel's future, Hosea returns to the shameful present. Gomer's life-style has provided him with ample material for a vivid description of Israel's "harlotry." Hosea's language is so personal and passionate one may conclude that he is pleading his own cause with his adulterous wife, but gradually it becomes clear that it is Yahweh who is urging the faithful of the nation to persuade their mother, Israel, to return to her former love and loyalty. What Hosea had experienced with his unfaithful wife, Gomer, Yahweh had experienced with unfaithful Israel. Chapter 2 presupposes that Gomer has already sunk deep into adultery, and it oscillates between the husband's longing to have her back and Yahweh's similar longings for Israel.

1. The Faithlessness of Israel (2:2-5)

The urgency of the appeal ("contend") is indicated by its repetition. Individual Israelites who are still sensitive to divine influence are the ones addressed. Let them "contend" with their mother, the nation, that she change her ways. Out of love for her they should work for her best interests. Yahweh renounces the relationship as husband and wife because of Israel's whoredoms. No such relationship can exist under conditions as they are. If a relation is to be sustained between them, Israel must put away "her adultery from between her breasts"; interpreted either as the wearing of jewelry between the breasts in honor of certain deities with whom the Israelites committed adultery (by forsaking Yahweh), or the adulterer who lies between the breasts is to be driven away.

Unless Israel turns from her idolatry, Yahweh will strip her of all that He has given her. Where wholehearted reconciliation does not take place, there is only one thing to do—to go through with the divorce proceedings. The procedure suggested here was well known as early as the middle of the second millennium B.C. The wife was compelled to leave everything in the husband's house—even her clothes, since he had provided them. This was true because the wife was considered a possession of the husband and everything she had belonged to him. Applied to Israel, this meant that Yahweh owned everything He had provided for her. Hence to be divorced by Him meant to be completely dispossessed, with nothing left but the naked body (v. 3). Israel then will become only "a wilderness," "a parched land" famishing from lack of rain (cf. Jer. 13:22, 26; Ezek. 16:38f; Lev. 20:10; Deut. 22:22).

The inhabitants of the land, "her children," will also suffer along with the mother because they are "children of harlotry" (v. 4). The phrase does not mean simply children born of a mother with unchaste tendencies, but children who themselves possess such tendencies and indulge in unchaste practices. They have endorsed the sin of their mother.

Israel's guilt is further described in verse 5, " ... mother hath played the harlot." Openly she had violated her obligations to Yahweh; such conduct is rightfully described as "shameful." Deaf to all exhortations, Israel had declared, "I will go after my lovers." These lovers were the Baalim, the gods of the native Canaanites. Israel's worship of these local gods arose first in connection with agriculture. These Baalim were thought to fertilize each his own district by his streams and springs, and hence came to be considered as the owners of those fertile spots. In time they were regarded also as sending the rain and were worshiped as the givers of fertility and prosperity. Gradually Israel came to view these Baalim as the source of "every good and perfect gift," and to pay them the homage belonging exclusively to Yahweh. And therein lay the "harlotry" so severely denounced by Hosea. For this disloyalty to Yahweh, Israel would be punished.

2. The Consequences of Israel's Infidelity (2:6-13)

This section contains two prophetic oracles united by a common purpose (to secure Israel's return to Yahweh), each of which is introduced by the expression "therefore" (see vv. 6, 9). Each oracle also delineates a specific response which the Lord makes to man's faithlessness.

a. Frustration and Despair (2:6-8)

Israel's determination to go after her lovers (v. 5) is matched with the Lord's equally resolute will that self-deception could not be allowed to prevail. Because of Israel's infidelity, Yahweh will act in such a way as to guarantee the redirection of her life, resulting in her devotion and fidelity. Rather than requiring the life of His wife (Israel), as the law specified, God's grace leads Him to seek to reorder her life. He accomplishes this by "hedging up her way" and "building a wall against her" (v. 6) that she may not pursue her accustomed way to meet her lovers. At first this discipline leads only to a more eager pursuit of them (v. 7), but she will not be able to "overtake them" or "find them." So in frustration and despair she resolves to "return to [her] first husband."

The sad note of Israel's return is found in the fact that "she did not know" (v. 8). As the ungrateful child fails to recognize abundant provisions from the parent's hand, so Israel failed to recognize in the abundance of her provisions the extended hand of Yahweh's blessing. And even worse, she had used these blessings as offerings to Baal. And because Israel did not recognize Yahweh as the true source of her blessings He will further discipline her by removing them from her.

b. The Penalty of Privation (2:9-13)

After the expression of hope for Israel's recognition of the true source of her blessings (v. 7c), Hosea's message of judgment continues. It should be noted, however, that his concept of judgment upon Israel is not her destruction, but the attempt to bring the nation to a consideration of the true source of her material abundance. To accomplish this Hosea affirms Yahweh's determination to "take back" or withhold His gifts of grain, wine, wool, and flax, perhaps by drought or the ravages of an invasion (v. 9). Israel will stand naked, hungry, and humiliated before the one she trusted (Baal), and her very condition will prove his inability to come to her aid (v. 10).

Further shame will be brought upon Israel because the mirth of their festivals—annual and monthly feasts and weekly sabbaths—will be no more (v. 11). Her vineyards and orchards—for which she had praised the Baalim as her hire for playing the harlot, but which were from Jehovah—will be as a forest and as a field for animals (v. 12). Israel will also be deprived (in judgment) of all the "feast days of the Baals" which she has observed, when she decked herself in festive finery and ornaments and became so absorbed in the wooing of her lovers that she completely forgot Yahweh (v. 13).

Those who cannot, or who will not, recognize the reality of God's gracious concern in their bounty (v. 8) will one day come to recognize it in the despair and privation of their want.

3. The Goal of Judgment: Renewal and Rebetrothal (2:14-23)

God's judgments are never merely punitive; rather, they are disciplinary for the purpose of turning the one punished into the divine way and will. Israel's futility and deprivation came upon her for the purpose of leading her back to Yahweh and to faithfulness in her covenant relationship with Him.

With these verses (14-15) it becomes more obvious that God's judgment upon Israel's iniquity is redemptive in purpose. The "therefore" of verse 14 may refer to the general sinful condition of Israel as described in verses 2-13. Such a situation requires divine intervention. It more likely refers to the last clause of verse 13. "Because Israel has forgotten me, therefore I *myself* [the Hebrew is emphatic] must make the advances; otherwise Israel will never repent and return to me" (free parapharase). The word *allure* is generally used in a bad sense, but not here. Better, "I will *woo* her and bring her into the wilderness."

Israel's early days in the wilderness came to be looked upon as the "honeymoon" of the Yahweh–Israel relationship (cf. Jer. 2:2). Now God will make love to Israel again "and bring her into the wilderness" on a second honeymoon. There in the wilderness with no other voice to be heard, Yahweh will "speak tenderly to her," a phrase more literally rendered, "speak to her heart." There He will also give back to Israel the vineyards which He had laid waste (v. 12), and "make the valley of Achor a door of hope" (v. 15). This valley on the northern boundary of Judah led up from Jericho to the hills of Judah. To this valley the Israelites had given the name *Achor,* that is, "trouble," or "troubling." It was here, after crossing the Jordan into Canaan, that Achan and his family were put to death for Achan's sin (Josh. 7:16ff). Just as significant as the death of Achan's family was the fact that "the Lord turned from his burning anger" (Josh. 7:26). Hosea used this experience not only to illustrate how the troubling of Israel (2:9ff) would become her door of hope, but also to make known that the Lord's anger was turned away from His people. Yahweh's purpose was to lead His people to a condition of renewal and hope that would result in the achievement of covenant faithfulness on Israel's part. That Yahweh's efforts were successful is indicated by Israel's response: "And there she shall answer as at the time when she came out of Egypt" (v. 15). Israel in the wilderness again will respond to Yahweh's wooing as she did in the somewhat idealistic age of the Exodus.

Renewed Israel will address Yahweh as *ishi,* literally "my husband," a word of tenderness (v. 16). *Baali* is a synonym of *ishi,* but it contains the word *Baal* ("master"), the name of a Canaanite deity. Hence it was associated with idolatry, and for this reason was rejected by Hosea. Neither were the Baalim to be mentioned by restored Israel (v. 17). The false gods of culture must give way to the sovereign Lord of history.

Another feature of this restored relationship between Yahweh and Israel will be peace between Israel and the animal world (v. 18). The wild beasts will no more ravage the land. Nature itself will be at peace with restored Israel. There will also be peace between Israel and other nations for Yahweh Himself "will abolish the bow, the sword, and war from the land" so that Israel can lie down with a feeling of complete confidence and security.

In love Yahweh tells His people, "I will betroth you to me forever" (v. 19). A second marriage between Yahweh and Israel—after her restoration—is portrayed as preceded by a second betrothal. It will not, like the first marriage at Sinai, be brought to an abrupt conclusion. It will endure "forever." The threefold repetition of *betroth* emphasizes not only the joy of the Bridegroom but the indissolubility of His choice. This new betrothal is "in righteousness and in justice." These words speak of the consistent dealings of God, who is no respecter of persons and who never acts unjustly, and of the demands and obligations of a service which God lays upon man. But more is needful if Israel is to be restored. Yahweh will also betroth her unto Him "in steadfast love and in mercy." The divine qualities of love and mercy must be exercised before Israel is betrothed to Yahweh "in faithfulness" (v. 20). It is not the bride's faithfulness that is referred to here but God's, that is, the constancy with which the new relations will be adhered to on His part. The permanency of the new betrothal depends more upon God than upon Israel.

As the result of God's actions ("I will betroth you") Israel will come to "know the Lord" (v. 20). This knowledge is not merely cognitive or intellectual, but knowledge growing out of a personal, living relationship—a communion of Yahweh with His people. It is significant to note that the word *know* is used of sexual relations in the Old Testament (e.g., Gen. 4:1). With that shared intimacy reserved only for marriage, Hosea fittingly pictures the depth of intimacy that will characterize the new relationship into which Yahweh will enter with His people. This is in striking contrast to the character of the old relationship which called forth from the prophet the stinging charge, "There is no knowledge of God in the land" (4:1), and, "My people are destroyed for lack of knowledge" (4:6).

The last three verses of the chapter (2:21-23) deal with the consummation of the marriage between Yahweh and Israel. Everything depends upon God. In the day of betrothal Yahweh "will answer the heavens" with His blessings (v. 21). They in turn will respond to the asking earth; the earth upon receiving the rain will respond to the vine, olive, and field asking for moisture; and all these will answer Jezreel ("God sows") (v. 22). Israel is now the people whom Yahweh *sows,* and not the people whom He *scatters* (cf. 1:4). The parallel continues in verse 23: Yahweh continues His *sowing,* and Lo-ammi (*Not my people*) now becomes "My people," whom Yahweh will provide for, bless, and protect. Thus cared for in this renewed covenant relationship, Israel will respond, "Thou art my God."

A word of caution may be apropos at this point lest one conclude that Hosea portrays Yahweh as practically forcing Israel against her will into this new relationship with Him. Nothing could be further from the prophet's purpose. Although it is evident that Hosea is emphasizing God's part in the process—because of His undying love for Israel—he most emphatically does not propose to teach that restoration and renewal can be experienced apart from the determination on Israel's part to return to the Lord (cf. 14:1-3). It is Hosea's view that God always takes the initiative in the work of redemption (and praise His name that He does!), but unless man responds in willing obedience, redemption will be incomplete. God may draw man with cords of love, but again if man fails to respond, salvation will be frustrated and the cords will be broken under the weight of God's judgment. It is only when Israel responds to the divine initiative of love that she will find her true good, which is His goodness alone.

QUESTIONS FOR DISCUSSION

1. In 2:2-13 is reference made to Gomer as Hosea's unfaithful wife or to Israel as the adulterous wife of Yahweh? Might the reference be to both Gomer and Israel? In what way(s) had Israel committed adultery toward Yahweh?

2. By way of contrast read Proverbs 31:10-31.

3. What punishment did the Old Testament law prescribe for an adulteress? (See Lev. 20:10.) Why did not Yahweh go to this same (rather) harsh extreme with His unfaithful wife, Israel?

4. Israel *was* punished for her unfaithfulness to Yahweh (see 2:6-8, 9-13). What was the purpose of God's judgment upon her? (See 2:14-20.) Are God's judgments always of such a nature? Does this in any way suggest that man is forced into the right relationship with God or that he is not free to choose his own way?

D. Hosea's Love for Gomer
Illustrative of God's Love for Israel (3:1-5)

A basic issue for the interpretation of this chapter is the relationship of chapters 1 and 3. Several questions are pertinent and some attempt must be made to answer them. Is the woman in chapter 3 Gomer or some other person? If she is Gomer, is chapter 3 an autobiographical account of identical events described by the prophet's biographer in chapter 1 (vv. 2-9)? Or, is chapter 3 the sequel to chapter 1 (and 2?), providing a description of the manner of Gomer's redemption following her unfaithfulness? It is difficult to answer these questions apart from an examination of the significance of the command to Hosea: "Go again, love a woman." There are two views relative to the position in the sentence of the Hebrew word translated "again": (1) It may be joined with the preceding words and translated as follows: "And the Lord said to me again: Go, love a woman. . . ." Such a translation implies that the woman referred to was some woman other than Gomer. (2) If the word *again* is joined with the words which follow, the translation will read: "And the Lord said to me: Again go, love a woman. . . ." In this case the woman of chapter 3 is none other than the Gomer of chapter 1, and chapter 3 is viewed as the sequel or continuation of the story related in chapter 1. That this latter view is the correct one is supported by two considerations: (1) The prophet is commanded to follow the example of the Lord, who loves the children of Israel though they have turned to other gods. In order to follow this example Hosea would have to continue loving the same woman since there is no indication whatsoever that Yahweh is going to love any spouse other than Israel. In fact, His unending love for Israel is the significant point of the entire experience; and, (2) it was the purpose of the writer to place the redemption of Gomer (vv. 1-3) and the parallel promise of hope for Israel (vv. 4-5) as the climax of the larger body of material found in Hosea 1–3.

1. Hosea Redeems His Unfaithful Wife (3:1-3)

In this act Hosea again represents himself as commanded by God, but his language must be interpreted as was done in chapter 1:2 (see Introduction, pp. 18-21). The prophet's love for his faithless and degraded wife moved him to redeem and reinstate her. Later he came to feel that this impulse was divinely implanted for the purpose of portraying to the nation the unchangeable love of Yahweh for His people. But before Hosea redeemed his wife he had come to the awareness of God's unquenchable love for the people of Israel "though they love other gods and love cakes of raisins" (delicacies made of pressed grapes used in idol worship). It was only under the compulsion of a love like Yahweh's love for Israel that Hosea could have redeemed his wife, described now as one "who is beloved of a paramour [unlawful lover] and is an adulteress"; a description which shows how great was the act of love demanded of the prophet.

The account of Gomer's redemption is forthright and simple (3:2), giving little evidence of the love and devotion which must have impelled Hosea to act as he did. Why Hosea had to buy back his wife is not told. The money must have been paid either to Gomer's paramour for the loss of his mistress, or to her owner, if indeed she was now a slave. The price paid was fifteen shekels of silver and a homer and a lethech of barley. Information concerning the value of these items is not sufficient to arrive at the purchase price of Gomer in dollars and cents. It is of significance to note that a female slave carried a value of thirty shekels (Exod. 21:32), and that the same value was set on the worth of a woman in calculating the fulfillment of a vow (Lev. 27:4). Such a price would fit the circumstances in this instance if Gomer was a slave or bound by a vow to some shrine.

In order to determine Gomer's dependability and steadfastness, Hosea at first isolated her so that she could not "play the harlot" (3:3). She was to remain in seclusion for an extended period of time. She must be unchaste no more and become no man's possession. The purpose of this seclusion and restriction was to teach Gomer to control her passions in preparation for resuming her former position as the prophet's wife. Meanwhile Hosea would treat her with compassion and love, protecting and providing for her, but claiming for himself none of a husband's privileges: "so will I also be to you" (3:3). Hosea did not seek mere possession but a response from the one he loved. He would not go in to her, for more than anything he wanted her to come to him. There is portrayed in these strange tactics the pathos and power of God's love—"a love that imprisons to set free, destroys false love for the sake of true, punishes in order to redeem."

2. The Message for Israel (3:4-5)

Verse 4 explains the actions of verse 3. Like Gomer, so Israel: as Gomer was deprived of her conjugal rights as a wife, so faithless Israel would be deprived of her civil and religious privileges. What went on in Hosea's house was symbolical, even prophetic, of what would be done to the nation. What Israel will be denied is itemized in a series of six things presented in related pairs. The first pair, king and prince, represent the entire royal institution. Hosea seems to have looked upon Israel's kings as a visible sign of their rebellion against Yahweh (cf. 5:1; 8:4; 10:15; 13:10ff.). The second pair, sacrifice and pillar, were elements associated with public worship. The manner and place of sacrifice were stressed in the law. Israel would be unable to meet these conditions during her period of probation. Pillars were cult objects used in pagan worship but forbidden to Israel (Deut. 16:22). The third pair of elements of which Israel will be deprived includes the ephod and teraphim, media used in searching out the future and often associated with prophecy. The exact meaning of ephod in its many uses in the Old Testament is not clear—ranging from linen vestment worn by the priest to an idol-image connected with the giving of oracles (cf. Exod. 28:12 with Judg. 18:14ff). There is a similar obscurity about the meaning and usage of teraphim. It is clear, however, that at one time they were looked upon as gods (Gen. 31:30; 1 Sam. 19:13, 16). Perhaps as a pair ephod and teraphim represented Israel's ritual for securing a divine revelation apart from the tradition or the prophetic message. Israel, then, will be stripped of king, cult, and divination.

The text is silent concerning both cause and circumstance that will culminate in this condition for Israel. Will it result from a deprived condition in their own land (2:6), to life in the wilderness (2:14), or to exile (9:3; 11:5)? The description leaves the matter open, and points rather to the removal of that which stood between Israel and her former true relation to Yahweh. But after these obstacles to that genuine relationship are removed, Israel will return to Yahweh (v. 5). Here the eschatalogical hope of Hosea is again expressed (cf. 1:10ff; 2:16ff). The prophet was enabled to face the severe disintegration of his day with the assurance born of faith that history would yet see the ultimate fulfillment of God's purposes for His people. Just as Hosea was confident that the period of punishment and separation to which he had condemned his wife would have the desired effect, he was equally sure that the experience of discipline Yahweh was to bring upon His wife (Israel) would lead her back in contrition and repentance.

Israel will return not only seeking her true husband,

the Lord of the Covenant, but "David her king" as well, that is, the reigning king of the line of David. It seems clear that Hosea expected all Israel, as one united family, to return to Yahweh and to the Davidic king. The two ideas are frequently found together in the prophetic material (e.g., cf. Jer. 30:9; Ezek. 34:23ff.; 37:24ff.). There is, to be sure, the strong possibility of Messianic implications in this verse (v. 5). However, the analogy of Amos 9:11 suggests that Hosea did not have in mind the person of the king but the dynasty itself; that is, "David" is equivalent to the representative of David. Israel's seeking after the Lord in fear and trembling is to occur "in the latter days." This phrase may simply mean later from the viewpoint of the prophet, that is, after Israel's period of separation and restriction is ended. Or it may refer to a golden age, the ideal or Messianic age, which is to follow the existing order. The former idea seems preferable here.

These three chapters (1–3) are very important, the most significant in the entire book. This is true not only because of their relationship to the book as a whole but also, and chiefly, because of the lesson of love contained in them. Hosea's love for his erring wife Gomer, yes; but more importantly Yahweh's love for His adulterous wife Israel. In these chapters the parallel between Hosea and Gomer and between Yahweh and Israel is clearly presented. Hosea's experience with Gomer parallels Yahweh's experience with the nation. Israel's sin was that of idolatry. She had committed spiritual adultery or "whoredom." As punishment the kingdom would be destroyed, the nation scattered (*Jezreel*). They would be without God's mercy (*Lo-ruhamah*) and not His people (*Lo-ammi*). Following a period of privation, Israel will repent, sown to Yahweh (*Jezreel*), and will become His people (*Ammi*) having obtained mercy (*Ruhamah*). Then the nation will seek Yahweh and under the leadership of one of David's line will enjoy the fullness of God's blessings.

Such, in brief, is the substance of the first division of Hosea's book. One feels in almost every line how the prophet's tragic experience with Gomer has indelibly stamped upon his inner being a sense of the heinousness of Israel's infidelity to Yahweh. Hosea's own unquenchable love for his "whoring" wife and his eager longing to win her back were but the shadow of Yahweh's mighty love for His people and of His insatiable desire to regain their wholehearted devotion. And with Yahweh desire is purpose and purpose is accomplishment, though it may be long delayed by human folly and obstinancy.

QUESTIONS FOR DISCUSSION

1. In chapter 3 whose love is magnified, Hosea's love for Gomer or Yahweh's love for Israel? (See Hos. 3:1; cf. 1 John 4:19.)
2. Was Hosea's action toward Gomer, following her purchase, for the purpose of punishing or redeeming her? How did she respond to the prophet? Do we know? What was Israel's response to Yahweh's gracious offers of pardon? Further study of Hosea will provide the answer.
3. What should be the response of a husband or wife toward an adulterous companion? Is divorce the only answer?
4. In what way(s) may it be said that Hosea's heartbreaking experience with Gomer proved a blessing in disguise?

Part Two
GOD'S WORD THROUGH HOSEA'S MESSAGES: REVELATION IN PROCLAMATION
(Hosea 4:1– 14:9)

In the second division of the book (chaps. 4–14) there is no direct reference to the circumstances of Hosea's life as previously mentioned (chaps. 1–3). But the same basic emphasis of the love of Yahweh for Israel and Israel's unfaithfulness to Yahweh constitutes the very warp and woof of the entire series of oracles. With burdened heart and bitter indignation at the sins of his people, the prophet stepped from the moral ruin of his own home into the environment of a degenerate people. The sins of those in all walks of life are exposed and censured. They are all traced to one source—the spirit of unfaithfulness toward Yahweh. The spiritual adultery of Israel is here portrayed in detail. It is a dark and dreadful picture in which warning is repeatedly given of the inevitable judgment which such conduct will bring upon the nation. Yet, in spite of all her sin, Yahweh stands ready to pardon and restore if Israel will only repent and return to Him.

Because of his experience with Gomer, Hosea was in a better position to observe the "whoredoms" of the nation toward its God. All about him he saw the beloved kingdom falling apart, its ideals gone, hastening toward destruction. It is not surprising, then, that impassioned feeling rather than logical arrangement is characteristic of the oracles comprising this part of the book. There is little logical connection among them. This is understandable when one realizes that in these chapters is found a tumultuous outburst of emotion from a heart surcharged with pity and scorned love. It is here that Hosea's personality is revealed, one that is distinctive among the prophets. "What Hosea gives us is really monologues, the ebullitions of a deeply moved heart, torn by grief in all its varying moods and sentiments. . . . But it is exactly this subjectivity and individuality which gives to the book . . . its special charm and irresistible efficacy."[1]

It is hardly possible to divide chapters 4–14 any further than that found in the chapter divisions themselves. In these chapters, aptly described as the "Lord's controversy with his people," one hears the noise of a nation falling into oblivion, the crumbling of a glorious past. Since "decay has no climax and ruin no rhythm," it comes as no surprise to find it next to impossible to delineate exact and workable subdivisions of Hosea's record of Israel's fall. But some division of this section must be attempted to facilitate its study. The writer hopes that the structure employed will prove to be our servant rather than our master.

A. The Lord's Controversy with His People (4:1–9:9)

Introduction: The Case Against the Nation (4:1-3)

This brief oracle (vv. 1-3) stands at the beginning of the second major section of the book which, in marked contrast to chapters 1–3, is composed entirely of miscellaneous messages of the prophet. It appropriately serves as an introduction to what follows with its opening summons to Israel to hear Yahweh's word, its comprehensive

---

1. Carl H. Cornill, *The Prophets of Israel* (Chicago: Open Court Publishing Co., 1897), p. 51.

statement of her guilt, and of the punishment to come upon the land. The particular type of prophetic-speech form to which this oracle belongs is that of the "judgment speech" (cf. Hos. 2:2; Mic. 6:1ff.; Isa. 1:18ff.). The source of this form is found in the legal procedure practiced in Israel's courts, and its use has the effect of putting the entire nation on trial with Yahweh serving as both prosecutor and judge. The Lord indeed has a "lawsuit with the inhabitants of the land." It is difficult to determine both the date and the occasion which called forth this brief oracle. It nevertheless contains a vivid summary of the situation which Hosea faced.

Yahweh charged His people first in negatives, using normative concepts for the conduct expected of Israel (v. 1b), and then positively by itemizing a series of crimes against the divine law (v. 2). This results in the most comprehensive picture possible of the sins of omission and commission—the portrayal of a people living in flagrant contradiction of their covenant relationship with Yahweh. Specifically they were accused of a lack of "faithfulness," "kindness," and "knowledge of God." All three are covenantal terms and must be understood in that context. *Faithfulness* in its original meaning signifies "truth, not only in the sense of speaking what is right, but also doing what is right." Its full sense is more nearly expressed by "faithfulness," "fidelity," or "steadfastness." Honesty, constancy, trustworthiness, and dependability are synonyms. The lack of these qualities in one's relationship with the Lord is destructive of any continuing basis of fellowship. Man can live with neither God nor man if their relationship is devoid of faithfulness. "Kindness" was equally wanting. This word in popular usage is a rather feeble word, connoting a mild type of consideration and concern for others. But the word used here (Heb., *hesed*) is a strong word, meaning "covenant love," which speaks of a relationship between two who have accepted mutual obligations in a spirit of trust

51

and steadfast love. This covenant love has a wide range of meanings, but in each instance of its use it is a love that is circumscribed and defined by the framework of a covenant relationship.

It is readily seen that truth and love are uniquely joined. Could Paul have had this uniqueness in mind when he wrote of "speaking the truth in love" (Eph. 4:15)? A statement ascribed to Jerome is pertinent: "Truth without love leads to hardness; love without truth to weakness."[2]

The root evil named in God's indictment against His people is the lack of a "knowledge of God in the land." To know God means for the prophet much more than passive acquaintance with or intellectual knowledge of Him. For Hosea, "to know" is to have intimate experience with, to share in a relationship at the deepest and most personal level of existence as, for example, in the marriage relationship (cf. Gen. 4:1, 17, 25). With the shared intimacy suggested by the consummation of a couple's love in marriage, the prophet delineates the depth of intimacy which should characterize the relationship between the Lord and His people. Such knowledge of God is prerequisite to faithfulness and kindness, rests upon a spiritual experience with God, and results in obedience to the moral laws of God.

Turning from the negative bases for God's controversy with Israel, Hosea now presents in positive fashion her sins of commission, a veritable flood of evils. In the Hebrew five infinitive absolutes, which emphasize and intensify the bare act of the verbs, itemize the dimension of Israel's guilt. Significantly the five crimes named (v. 2) are more than simple violations of general morality; they are acts prohibited by the tradition in Israel which summarized the will of Yahweh under His covenant with

2. Roy L. Honeycutt, "Hosea," *Broadman Bible Commentary* (Nashville: Broadman Press, 1972), p. 21.

Israel. Consequently these acts (swearing, lying, killing, stealing, committing adultery) violated five of the Ten Commandments which are most directly related to man's relationship with his fellowman. The multiplicity of such deeds indicates that Israel had sunk to the level of a chaotic society which had no recognizable regard for the divine law. Social violence had become a way of life as one bloody deed followed another.

The ill effects of such faithlessness are shown to have affected the totality of Israelite life (v. 3). Even the land mourns, as do the beasts of the field, birds of the air, and fish of the sea. Although Hosea makes use of a drought-vocabulary in describing the catastrophe that has come upon the land, he is probably not referring to an actual drought, or of devastation of the land wrought by the Assyrians or by internal political disorder. Rather, he views Israel's violation of the covenant faith as having brought a curse upon the land over which man had been given dominion (Gen. 1:26ff.). Now this land has been polluted by its inhabitants and shares God's curse upon them. When God's people break covenant, all of creation suffers the consequences of their sin (see Gen. 8:21; Rom. 8:19ff.).

1. Spiritual Unfaithfulness and Moral Decay (4:4–7:2)

After presenting in 4:1-3 a somewhat general indictment of the nation of Israel for its wickedness, Hosea now turns and deals in more specific fashion with moral defection in certain areas of national life and worship.

a. God's Case Against the Priests (4:4-10)

One indication of widespread moral deterioration in Israel was the corruption of her priesthood. These verses provide a vivid description of a degenerate priesthood which will bring upon priest and people alike the judgment of God.

The terminology used in verse 4 ("contend" and "contention") serves to link this passage with the preceding verses. This verse is difficult, but the meaning derived from the Revised Standard Version is adequate: "Let no one contend or complain, because the people are not to blame; my controversy is with the priests." Furthermore, the priests (and prophets) stumble by day and night, that is, continuously (v. 5). Those who were the spiritual leaders and to whom the people looked for guidance were not fit to lead others, since each stumbled in his walk or way. They were the religious officials whose duty it was to lead and instruct the people; but how could they, when so guilty of evil themselves? The covenant faith which the priests should have maintained had been ignored by the very ones charged to teach it. The meaning of the term "your mother" is much disputed. But whether it refers to the nation Israel (cf. 2:2, 5) or to the stock, clan, or family of priests, the end result is the same—destruction of the priests and priesthood.

In verse 6 Hosea again turns to the theme of the "knowledge" of God (see on v. 1). Since the religious teachers had failed to do their duty, the people are "destroyed for lack of knowledge." This fate is so certain as to be characterized by the use of a Hebrew verb form indicating a completed state of action. The priests are not only called to account for not instructing the people in the "knowledge" of God, but they are charged with rejecting that knowledge themselves. And because the priests have despised and scorned this knowledge and forgotten God's law (instruction, revelation), God will divest them of their priesthood and will forget their sons in that the normal succession in the priestly line will cease with the destruction of the kingdom of Israel. Those who reject the knowledge of God are rejected by Him.

Verses 7-8 continue the prophet's theme of the irresponsibility of the priests. They were increasing in both numbers and affluence, for it was a time of unparalleled prosperity. However, instead of enhancing the religious institutions and improving the teaching of the will and way of God, they showed further deterioration in their responsibility as spiritual leaders. For "the more they increased [in numbers and wealth], the more they sinned against [the Lord]." Since the priests are unworthy of their office, the Lord "will change their glory into shame." Their glory was the privilege of service for the Lord and His people. But instead of providing the right kind of leadership and instruction for the nation, they actually fed on its sin, greedily anticipating the iniquity of its citizens. The priest's livelihood was derived through his sharing a part of the sacrifice brought by the worshiper (see Lev. 6:18, 29; 7:6). The more the people sinned, the greater the number of sacrifices, and the greater profit to the priests. Hence the priests, moved by mercenary motives, encouraged the people to sin. When religious leaders stoop so low, it is not surprising that Hosea's next word is one of judgment!

When God's judgment comes, the priests need not hope, because of their position or office, to receive a lesser punishment. "It shall be like people, like priest" (v. 9a), that is, the priests will fare just like the people. Or stated another way, in the day of judgment there will be no spiritual or moral equivalent of the 10 percent ministerial discount. Religious leaders will in no way escape the righteous demands which God makes of religious workers and people alike.

God's punishment upon the priests in each instance is related to the form in which the rebellious spirit expressed itself in their lives (v. 10). They will eat their fill of the sin offerings of the people, but they will not be satisfied. They will continue to engage in intercourse with sacred prostitutes in the cultic ceremonies in order to set in motion cosmic procreative powers to assure

55

fertility of soil and people,[3] but this, too, will be of no avail. The point here is the total lack of satisfaction and complete futility of religious leaders who sacrifice their holy calling at the altar of greed and sensuality. The final sentence of verse 10 gathers all the charges against the priests into one final summary of complaint: "They have forsaken the Lord to cherish harlotry." One sees here a strong contrast between the Lord and harlotry, which, for Hosea, stood for the popular and paganized religious practices he so strongly condemned. The prophet's complaint is that instead of practicing the covenant obligations of "faithfulness, covenant love, and knowledge of God," they have observed the ceremonies and religious rites of Baal.

b. God's Case Against the Cult (4:11-14)

Here Hosea attacks the people for certain religious practices that reveal their moral defection and the extent of their infidelity to the covenant God. These verses are related to the previous ones (4-10) since they deal with the consequences to the people of the priests' corruption. "Whoredom"—both idolatry and the licentious acts that were associated with the cult (worship)—combined with intoxication to take away "the understanding" (literally, *heart,* the center of the will and understanding in Hebrew psychology); thus, the people are prevented from acting with discretion and discernment. Liquor and lust have combined to confuse and enfeeble their minds.

The cult (worship) of Hosea's day had become degenerate. Drink offerings were turned into occasions for drunkenness. "My people inquire of a thing of wood, and their staff gives them oracles" (v. 12). They sought oracles from lifeless wood in contrast to the powerful

---

3. The sexual motif is basic to the understanding of this passage. See Roy L. Honeycutt, "Hosea," pp. 3f.

living God. The staff refers to some form of divination in which a stick is thrown in order to secure the answer of the deity from the way it falls (cf. Ezek. 21:21f.). Such practices were useless, of course, but a spirit of harlotry had so taken hold of the people that they were led astray (v. 12). They were so obsessed with the sensuous appeal of the fertility rites of the cult that they had lost all sense of moral judgment. Blinded by these things they had "left their God to play the harlot"; that is, they were engaged in religious adultery with its heinous immoralities.

Hosea does not condemn the sacrificial worship at the high places ("mountains and hills") as such, but rather the identification of that worship with the licentious worship of Baal, including the practice of prostitution in the shade of the trees. Even their daughters and brides did the same (v. 13). Though adulteresses were severely dealt with (see Lev. 20:10) in Israel, the prophet declares that the Lord will not punish the daughters and brides for their illicit deeds, for the blame for such conduct lies elsewhere (v. 14). The men themselves are guilty, the fathers and teachers of their families. Overwhelmed by the spirit of harlotry inherent in the nature cult, they commit adultery with prostitutes outside the cult ("harlots") as well as those within it (v. 14). This passage is significant in that it is one of only a few in the Old Testament which places men on the same level of responsibility as women. Hosea was the first prophet to attack the double standard—a separate standard for men and women. It is impossible for the men of a nation to live on a different and lower moral level than its women, and yet expect their daughters and wives to live up to a higher standard of moral purity. The prophet had no place for a permissive sexual ethic. Rather, he proposes that God will judge men on the same basis as women; there is no such thing as a double sexual ethic.

Consequently the entire nation is brought under a

sentence of condemnation due to its deviations from covenant obligations inherent in its relationship with Yahweh. This is clear from the proverb with which verse 14 closes. A people devoid of the power of understanding—that is, discernment and discrimination—will inevitably "come to ruin." The Hebrew word for *ruin* occurs only two other times in the Old Testament (see Prov. 10:8, 10 margin) and suggests incapacity as the result of lameness or illness. Hence the indication that a people lacking the capacity to discern the way of the Lord and to follow that way is religiously sick unto death unless restoration takes place.

c. Words of Warning to Judah (4:15-19)

These verses, and others referring to Judah (e.g., 1:7, 11; 4:15; 5:10-14; 8:14), are viewed by certain critics as non-Hoseanic and all such references are described as "additions by a later hand." Their evidence for this conclusion is not convincing. Until more convincing arguments are presented, it is preferable to consider such passages as genuine oracles of Hosea. It seems most logical to conclude that he had an intimate knowledge of conditions in the kingdom of Judah, that he had a deep concern for her, and that because of this concern he desired only the very best for Judah—whether his words to her were favorable or not. Further, in the prophet's warnings and promises to Judah there was contained a message to Israel, if she would only hear and heed.

Hosea's warning to Judah is a threefold one. In the first place, she should not become like Israel, particularly in her worship life and experiences. Israel is hopeless, a captive to a spirit of harlotry (v. 17). Let not Judah be caught in the same trap. Whether or not worshipers from Judah were visiting Gilgal and Bethel, two of Israel's principle cultic centers, is of little significance. Hosea's vigorous exhortation to Judah not to visit these favorite shrines in Israel is nonetheless a bitter condemnation of their cult meant for the ears of those who did worship there.

Although there were two sites in Israel identified by the name Gilgal, the one located in the Jordan Valley "on the east border of Jericho" (Josh. 4:19) is probably the one mentioned. Beth-aven ("house of evil") is a scornful nickname for Beth-el ("house of God"). This was especially appropriate since one of Israel's two golden calves was housed in the shrine at Bethel and worshiped there. Further, Judah is not to swear, "As the Lord lives." Though swearing of this kind was permissible (see Deut. 6:13; 10:20), yet the oath had its roots in the fear of the Lord and not in idolatry. Worshiping at the seats of idolatry, Gilgal and Bethel, and swearing in the name of God were not compatible.

A second warning to Judah is to not become like Israel in her willful disobedience to God (v. 16). Israel had repeatedly rebelled against Yahweh. Like a stubborn heifer which always resists and then plunges in the direction opposite to that in which she is pushed, Israel had perversely gone contrary to the Lord's way for her (cf. Jer. 31:18). Since Israel had so decisively rejected God's offers of guidance and direction, how could He pasture her "like a lamb" in a wide place? One simply cannot treat a stubborn heifer and a gentle lamb in the same manner. No herdsman can lead a stubborn herd into luxuriant and luscious pastures if it refuses to follow. Neither can the Lord feed Israel in pleasant pastures, for she will not follow Him. Judah, beware! Do not be stubborn like Israel.

Hosea's third warning to Judah is to leave Israel alone (v. 17). How best respond to a people "joined to idols," "a band of drunkards," given to "harlotry," and who "love shame [harlotrous practices] more than their glory" (decent worship in the service of their Lord)? The prophet's advice to Judah is both pointed and pertinent:

Leave them alone! In this verse there occurs for the first time in Hosea the name "Ephraim" for Israel. Ephraim was the largest and most important tribe of the ten included in the northern kingdom. Hosea uses this term for Israel thirty-seven times—more often than any other writer in the Old Testament. Ephraim is *joined* or *mated* to idols as a wife is *joined* to her husband (see Mal. 2:14, "companion"). Israel is so bound to her idols that there is no hope. Long addiction to sinful worship has made reconciliation impossible. The faithful of Judah, then, are warned not to endanger their own safety by coming in contact with idolatrous Ephraim. Leave her alone!

It should be pointed out, however, that to interpret this passage as meaning God will utterly abandon and finally destroy Israel is highly inconsistent with the ultimate teaching of the prophet (cf. 1:10-11; 2:15; 11:8; 14:4-8).

The prophet concludes his warning to Judah with a poetic metaphor of judgment, "A wind has wrapped them [Israel] in its wings" (v. 19). The metaphor is that of a violent storm in which the wind has caught up the people in its currents ("wings") and drives and buffets them irresistibly in the direction in which it blows. *Ruach* is translated both "spirit" and "wind." The people of Israel of their own choice have been caught up in a "spirit [*ruach*] of harlotry" (see 4:12; 5:4). Now they will be enveloped in the "wind" (*ruach*) of God's judgment and swept into exile. The prophet is so certain of the judgment that he expresses it as having already occurred by using in the Hebrew the verb tense of completed action (the prophetic perfect.) When swept into exile, Israel "shall be ashamed because of their altars" in that they will discover the inadequacy of their gods and the pagan rites associated with them to effect deliverance. This is the acid test of religion. The true nature of pagan gods is clearly revealed in a crisis. They cannot keep the storm from enveloping their devotees in its

60

wings, or provide strength and hope in the midst of the storm as can God (cf. Isa. 46:1-5; Ps. 46:1ff.).

QUESTIONS FOR DISCUSSION

1. The second major division of Hosea (4:1– 14:9) is extremely difficult to subdivide. What explanation(s) can you give for this difficulty? (See Introduction for help on this question.)
2. Why did Hosea denounce the sacrificial worship (ritual) of his time? Was he opposed to the offering of sacrifices? Is it possible to have public worship without a ritual of some kind?
3. Distinguish between ritual and cult. Look up the meaning of both words in a dictionary.
4. Of what possible benefit to Israel were Hosea's warnings to Judah in 4:15-19?
5. In the context of 4:6-10 what is meant by Hosea's statement "And it shall be like people, like priest; I will punish them for their ways"? When the religious leaders of a nation are corrupt, is there any way or hope for the nation to escape moral decay?

---

d. The Treachery of All Ephraim (5:1-7)

(1) Condemnation of her collective leadership (5:1-2). "Hear this" (v. 1) points back to chapter 4, and relates what follows to what has been said. Corruption is rampant in all phases of Israel's life, making her punishment inevitable. It has been made clear already that the priests failed to discharge their duties (4:4ff.). It was

because of their failure that the nation was in such grave peril. And because they are most blameworthy they are the first addressed. Next comes the "house of Israel," that is, representatives of the people, or perhaps elders of the house of Israel, who are called to account. Finally the "house of the king" (royal court) is urged to give attention to the prophet's message. Hosea's catalog of leadership includes the dominant elements in Israel's society, men who held in their hands the nation's destiny. Hosea correctly affirms that "the judgment pertains to them," that is, to those groups judgment (right decisions, justice) had been committed. But they had failed to execute judgment; now God will do so, and they will be the recipients of it.

These who should have led the nation in ways of righteousness have become instead a "snare at Mizpah," a "net spread upon Tabor," and "have made deep the pit of Shittim" (vv. 1b-2a). The exact significance of these locations is not readily apparent, though they were connected with "high places" and as such had cultic significance. It is probable that Hosea referred to sites at which either contemporary or former leaders had led Israel into the worship of false gods. Three ways to catch wild animals are named: snare, net, and pit. These represent the seductions to idolatry by the leaders of Israel, religious snares by which the people were caught when they thought they were worshiping the Lord.

As the outworking of God's judgment (noted above), these same snares will catch those who set them as well as those who perhaps unwittingly fall into them. For the Lord will "chastise" all classes who are guilty. God has no favorites. The fact that a man is a priest or a king does not protect or excuse him. In verse 2b there is a ray of hope for Israel. Although "chastise" is an adequate translation, the Hebrew word used here is also used in the context of teaching and its discipline (cf. Deut. 8:5; Prov. 19:18; 31:1; Isa. 28:26). Thus Hosea suggests the idea of a redemption which is grounded in discipline. Though the leaders have failed and the people are not without fault, Yahweh remains their teacher. Through the discipline of history He will teach them the meaning of their status as the people of God, for whom punishment is not for the purpose of destruction but for salvation and deliverance (cf. 2:14ff.).

(2) Her incapability of returning to Yahweh (5:3-7).
Israel's moral failure is due to her turning away from God. It can be rectified only by returning to Him. But it is possible for a people to become so hardened by sin that they are incapable of repentance. Their sins, like a fetter, cling to their wills and they have no inclination to seek after God. They are in bondage, as addicted to sin as the addict is to his heroin. How true this was of the nation Israel!

Yet all of the time Yahweh is aware of His people's inability to return to Him and the reasons for it, inasmuch as He knows Ephraim, and Israel is not hidden from his eyes (v. 3). The first reason for her failure to return is due to the "spirit of harlotry" that is within her which results in Israel's "playing the harlot" (vv. 3-4). The spirit of harlotry had taken hold of the nation and its people were so obsessed by the sensuous appeal of the fertility rituals that they had lost all sense of moral judgment. As a result there was no longer any knowledge of God, without which it is impossible to achieve communion with Him. The spirit of harlotry in Israel further resulted in deeds which did not permit her to return to God. Israel is held captive in the grip of past deeds—those fateful blunders committed during her history in the land, which have shaped character so completely that, like an insurmountable wall, they now surround her. Israel's depravity is so total that return is humanly impossible apart from God's action in judgment to rescue her.

Another obstacle to Israel's return to the Lord is her pride. Some see in "the pride of Israel" (v. 5) a reference to Yahweh. Others view it as descriptive of the nation as self-willed, haughty, arrogant, that is, prideful. (The latter idea is preferable.) Such was Israel's true condition and it testified "to her face." Her own character and conduct give the most telling witness against her. By her confidence in the fertility cult to bring blessing, and by her avid desire to participate in immoralities associated with it, Israel gives incontrovertible evidence against herself in the trial before Yahweh. Her punishment will come out of her sin; she shall stumble and fall, for its (the cult's) failure will destroy her. In approaching Yahweh as though He were Baal, they cut themselves off from His blessings.

A third obstacle to Israel's return to God is her superficial worship (v. 6). Measured by the standards of men, religion in eigth-century Israel was highly successful. Worship centers thronged with people, and multiplied sacrifices were offered. The shrines overflowed with the sound of music and holy days were observed with careful detail (cf. Amos 5:21ff.). Thus Israel attempted to approach God through multiplied sacrifices and offerings, treating Him as though He were a Baal to be satisfied and sought after through a pagan cult. But "they will not find him; he has withdrawn from them." Finding the Lord in worship is dependent upon the manner of one's seeking. Israel sought God on occasions with a superficial commitment, at times with improper motives, and all too often guilty of personal conduct which contradicted the reality of a serious search for Him. They failed to find Him for He had withdrawn. Their lives had forced them out of the relationship essential for a return to God.

A final hindrance to Israel's return to God is her faithlessness (v. 7). In their apostasy the people of Ephraim have acted treacherously toward the Lord; but worse, they have fathered strange children, that is, produced a generation of children who do not know the Lord. As Gomer had borne children of whoredom to Hosea, so Israel had borne strange children to Yahweh. They have not been faithful in instructing their children in the covenant faith. Now it is impossible for the children to return to Yahweh. Consequently they have destroyed the household of faith and robbed their children of their rightful blessings in the covenant relationship with God. This was a serious indictment against the nation, and judgment would not be long in coming. In fact, the next "new moon," a celebrated festive occasion, would witness their own destruction and that of their "fields" (land divided or apportioned to Israel). How ironical, to be destroyed during the observance of a sacred day! (Cf. Amos 9:1ff.)

e. The Crisis of Civil War (5:8-14)

Israel's inability to return to Yahweh because of the spirit of harlotry within (5:3ff.) provides us with a plausible and logical reason for the presence at this point of a series of oracles unified by the common threat of danger to the nation from without. God has failed to secure a response through seeking to work within the hearts of the people. Perhaps a response will come in the light of His action from without.

It is now generally accepted that the events of this section (5:8-14) are directly connected with the history of the Syrian-Ephraimite war (735-33 B.C.). Throughout its course it was a venture fraught with folly and grievous consequences for the sister nations of Israel and Judah. Israel's King Pekah, faced with invasion by Tiglath-pileser of Assyria, joined forces with Rezin, king of Syria, against their common enemy (2 Kings 16:5; Isa. 7:1-2). In order to force Judah's participation in their coalition, the two kings laid siege to Jerusalem

(2 Kings 15:37), after taking certain border outposts including Gibeah, Ramah, and Beth-aven (Bethel). Meanwhile, Judah's King Ahaz had secured help from none other than Tiglath-pileser himself who, when he came to Judah's aid, moved against Israel in 733 B.C., reducing her to a state of near total insignificance.

With pressure from Israel relieved by the action of Tiglath-pileser, Judah retaliated against Israel and sought to regain the border cities of Gibeah, Ramah, and Bethel. Hence the words of warning to the three cities (v. 8). Hosea was certain that this fratricide would eventually result in Israel's punishment and desolation: "I declare what is sure" (v. 9).

Judah, no less than Ephraim, is deserving of punishment: Her princes "have become like those who remove the landmarks" (v. 10). In Israel these were sacred, for they marked the allotment of the land as God's gift (Deut. 19:14). The removal of landmarks was forbidden (Deut. 27:17) and was looked upon with contempt in the Old Testament (cf. Prov. 22:28; Mic. 2:2; Job 24:2). With these words (v. 10a) Hosea reduces Judah's retalitory invasion of Ephraim to the dimension of a guilty act of one covenant brother against another. Judah is therefore put under curse and the Lord will pour out His wrath upon them (v. 10b). Judah, as Ephraim, was guilty of futile efforts to gain security short of trust in Yahweh, the covenant God. In the historical period before us, she turned to Assyria (2 Kings 16:7ff.) and ignored the advice of Isaiah (Isa. 7:3ff.).

Israel and Judah alike were guilty; both were guilty of sins against the other, both trusted pagan Assyria for help in internal and external crises. Hosea understood what such a course of action meant for both nations. The Assyrian king could not heal their wounds or rid them of their festering sores (v. 13). Each had wounds too serious to be cured by such means, nor could God's judgment be averted by political solutions. Moral and spiritual sickness needs a moral and spiritual remedy. The only hope for Israel (and Judah) is a turning back to God from within the nation itself. The nation which has turned from God must repent and return to Him, so that He can reform it inwardly.

In a rather strange pair of similes, Hosea represents the Lord as the enemy within Israel ("like a moth" or "like dry rot," v. 12) and the enemy without ("like a lion," v. 14). Moths and rottenness work slowly, silently, but they destroy completely. History contains within itself the seeds of judgment, and there is constantly at work in history the silent and certain process of judgment. But at the same time the threat of a lion hangs heavy over the two kingdoms; Yahweh stalks His covenant people, and when the "king of the jungle" crouches over his prey, who would dare try to deliver it?

Thus the prophet lays bare the utter futility of seeking help and health by basing national politics on Assyrian might. To do so is merely dealing with symptoms and not the disease. Yahweh, not Assyria, is the ultimate source of their wound (vv. 12, 14), and He alone can heal them.

QUESTIONS FOR DISCUSSION

1. In 5:3 the designation "Ephraim" is used the second of thirty-seven times in this book for the northern kingdom of Israel (first used in 4:17). How explain or account for this usage?

2. Hosea seems to use in synonymous fashion the terms "turn" or "return to God" and "repentance." In 5:4-6 the prophet gives three reasons why it is impossible for Israel to turn to God or to repent. Locate these

reasons. Under what conditions is it impossible for a man to repent of his sins?
3. Why was the removal of landmarks considered a serious crime in Old Testament times?
(See Deut. 19:14; 27:17.)

f. The Futility of Insincere Repentance (5:15–6:6)

As a lion returning from the destruction of its prey,
the Lord will return to His place (v. 15). He will do so
because Israel has refused to repent and return to Him.
On His seat in heaven (or perhaps at Sinai) He will remain until such time as Israel shall seek Him with sincere
repentance, acknowledging their sins as they return.
With the victories of the Assyrian armies many people
came to believe that the Lord had indeed forsaken His
people. This is exactly what the prophet affirms. They
had rejected God, hence He lets them suffer the fate of
their own choosing. Meanwhile God awaits the time
when, out of their suffering, Israel will sincerely seek
Him. Hosea's announcement of Yahweh's withdrawal
"to my place" interprets God's wrath in such manner
that Israel's very punishment becomes an invitation to
repentance. This is a constant theme in Hosea, namely,
that God in His anger against His people's sin seeks their
ultimate reconciliation.

A defeat such as Israel suffered in the Syro-
Ephraimitic war might well have caused deep reflection
and soul-searching on Israel's part. There may well have
been some pangs of conscience preparatory to a genuine
mood of repentance. But did the quality of repentance
Israel showed compare favorably with that quality of
repentance which God requires? The answer to this question is dependent upon one's interpretation of verses

1-3. Some interpret this exhortation as a prayer of the people in earnest appeal to one another that they return to the Lord. Since He has "torn" and "stricken," He will "heal" and "bind up" and that right soon, that is, two or three days. The people now recognize that they must know and follow Jehovah; repentance and the knowledge of God are indissolubly bound together. When God sees a repentance effected through the knowledge of Himself, He will "revive," "raise up," and make to "live before him." Not only will He bestow these blessings, but He will shower favors upon them as of the heavy winter rains and the latter rains before harvest.

Others would add the word "saying" after 5:15 (see RSV) giving the reading, "In their distress they seek me, *saying* come, let us return to the Lord. . . ." This reading indicates an attitude far short of a deep and heartfelt repentance. It seems more akin to a hasty resolution from which a free and full confession of sin was notably absent. It was a repentance resulting from distress rather than from a deep sense of sin which had caused the distress. As such it was not genuine. Such an interpretation correctly relates verses 1-3 to verses 4-6 and is in complete harmony with the latter passage.

These verses (6:4-6) reveal the Lord's response to Israel's show of shallow repentance and humble return to His service. He finds nothing in their "liturgy of repentance" (vv. 1-3) of that costly repentance which demands confession of sin and the repudiation of faithless ways. Therefore He cries, "O Ephraim . . . O Judah, what shall I do with you?" The source of God's cry of anguish is not difficult to locate. Israel's love is as fleeting as a morning cloud or as the dew which quickly vanishes before the scorching sun (v. 4b). What indeed could be done with a people—Israel and Judah—whose love or loyalty was thus lacking in dependability? And because this love had been in the past as transient as a summer cloud, Yahweh had "hewn them by the prophets," that is, had sought to "fashion" their lives by the teachings of the prophets according to His will and way. Yahweh had also sent forth His "judgments" to illumine the dark paths of Israel's pilgrimage. These judgments of God were given to Israel from of old and were repeated and applied by prophet and priest with a single purpose in mind, to guide the nation in her covenant obligations as they related to God and neighbor.

God's judgments, then, were the shining lights by which Israel was to direct her ways and provided the basis of her covenant relationship with Yahweh and with her fellowman as well. Israel, however, had sought to make ritual observances the sole basis of this relationship. So, in another of His judgments God made known through the prophet Hosea that He desired "steadfast love and not sacrifice, the knowledge of God, rather than burnt offerings" (v. 6). (For discussion of "steadfast love" and "knowledge of God," see comment on 4:1.) "Steadfast love" (*hesed*) means the attitudes and deeds that faithfully maintain and enhance a relationship within the bonds of a mutual agreement, in Hosea's case Yahweh's covenant with Israel. The "knowledge of God" signifies much more than the idea of passive acquaintance or intellectual knowledge. It is rather that intimate, personal relationship with Him resulting in an attitude which makes for hearing and obeying His instruction.

Verse 6 is a famous sentence, one of the most sublime thoughts in the Old Testament, for with it Hosea laid bare the essence of real religion—relationship not ritual—and once for all made religion a matter of the heart. Christ gave added significance to this verse by referring to it on two occasions (Matt. 9:13; 12:7). Hosea had no intention of setting aside ceremonial religion, for in some form ceremony must always enter into man's worship of God. The words describe the mutual relation of moral obedience and ceremonial observance with respect to their comparative value, and declare unequivocally the superiority of the moral when it conflicts with the ceremonial (cf. 1 Sam. 15:22; Jer. 7:22-23; Mic. 6:6-8).

g. A geography of guilt (6:7–7:2)

What can Yahweh do with His people whose land can be described in terms of a geography of sin and guilt? When He prepares to forgive and restore them, He is confronted with a nation empty of repentance, whose evil deeds "encompass them" and like a company of witnesses unite to testify against them.

The sins enumerated in 6:7-10 are presented as evidence that Israel lacks the essential qualities which Yahweh requires in her relationship with Him (6:6). This section has been referred to as a sort of "miniature guidebook" to the geography of Israel's sin and guilt. Hosea moves from one location to another as he catalogs the notorious crimes which serve as an indictment against his beloved country. Interpretation of this section is not without its problems. In addition to difficulties related to the text itself, one is confronted with the problem that the incidents which were infamous in Hosea's day are now unknown or at best uncertain.

The first sin in Hosea's bill of indictment of Israel is a case of covenant violation (v. 7). "Adam" may also be translated "like Adam" or "like men" (KJV), but the adverb "there" as well as the parallel place names which follow ("Gilead," "Shechem," etc.) seem to validate the translation of "Adam" as a place name (RSV). A city named Adam is mentioned in Joshua 3:16, located on the Jordan River at the spot where the waters were cut off in order that Israel might cross over. Although the specific nature of covenant violation is not given, reference to this ancient site suggests that covenant breaking (infidelity) was nothing new in Israel's experience.

The city of Gilead is next in Hosea's catalog of Israel's sins (v. 8). Though the name is usually applied to a mountainous region east of the Jordan River, the prophet may have shortened a name such as Ramoth-Gilead. "City of evildoers, tracked with blood" gives little information as to sins committed there. From the reference in 2 Kings 15:25 that fifty men from Gilead aided Pekah in the murder of King Pekahiah, Hosea may be suggesting that political intrigue and revolt were also characteristic of Israel.

Shechem is the third city named by Hosea. This time, however, no charge is brought against the city itself but against groups of priests who "murder on the way to Shechem" (v. 9). The reasons for such murder on the part of priests is not clear. Shechem was not an official state shrine as were Dan and Bethel. Perhaps priests of the state cult went to the extreme of murdering worshipers on the way to a rival shrine as a method of killing competition.

The final item of Hosea's indictment deals with the whole house of Israel rather than a particular place (v. 10). This inclusiveness is perhaps indicative of the fact that the previous specific charges were but examples of a guilt which was common to the entire nation. Some have suspected that "house of Israel" has been substituted for an original "Bethel" ("house of God"). Since Hosea's theme of harlotry has a definite cultic setting, such an indictment would be most appropriate. Nevertheless, Yahweh cries out in utter astonishment at what He sees there—"a horrible thing . . . harlotry." Bethel was a royal shrine established by Jeroboam I who placed a golden calf at its center. No wonder "Israel is defiled"! A moral defilement for which Israel must bear the blame is discovered in the nation. Even Judah had not escaped the infection. So to her also a harvest of punishment is appointed; what Judah has sown, that shall she also reap (v. 11a).

In the midst of an environment described by the

above catalog of sins a divine lament bursts forth over the impasse created by the Lord's willingness to forgive His people and their complete identification with evil. "What shall I do with you, O Ephraim?" (6:4). What indeed shall God do with His people? They fail to remember the history of Yahweh's revelation, but He remembers the history of their sin (7:2). Now their deeds surround them as prison walls; what they have done, they have become. Sins do not disappear with the mere passage of time. They live on to accuse men in the present. Forgiveness and "forgottenness" result only from sincere repentance and confession.

In this section (4:1–7:2) Hosea portrays a people on the toboggan slide of moral decay rapidly moving toward a ruinous collision with the moral judgments of God. Symptoms of this moral sickness abounded; in the king's court, shrine, and simple homes of the land, immoralities prevailed. The sinfulness of Israel was without end. Every effort to redeem them only discovered more of it. Real repentance was impossible. They seemed to have lost the capacity to do so. As the prophet declared, "Their deeds do not permit them to return to their God" (5:4).

In giving so thorough an indictment of the moral anarchy in Israel, it would be strange indeed if Hosea had stopped short of treating the political folly and national restlessness which resulted from it. This is done in the next division.

QUESTIONS FOR DISCUSSION

1. What evidence is there in 5:15–6:4 that Israel's repentance is insincere? Contrast the spirit of Israel's repentance in these verses with that of King David in Psalm 51.

2. It has been said that with the statement in 6:6, Hosea "laid bare the essence of real religion—relationship not ritual—and once for all made religion a matter of the heart." Explain. What use did Christ make of the thought expressed in 6:6 (see Matt. 9:13; 12:7)? Is not man constantly in danger of substituting ritual for righteousness or a personal relationship with God? (Illustrate by giving examples.) Check the thought expressed in 1 Samuel 15:22.

3. According to Hosea's "miniature guidebook" to the geography of Israel's sin and guilt (6:7–7:1), what notorious crimes had Israel committed in days past which so vitally affected her present relationship with Yahweh?

4. Compare Amos 5:21-23 and Isaiah 1:11-14 with Hosea 6:6. What is the central idea in each passage? Is it the same for all three? A look at Amos 5:24 and Isaiah 1:15-17 will help in finding the answer.

2. Political Instability and Continued Unfaithfulness (7:3–9:9)

With the beginning of this section one notes a new emphasis in Hosea's prophecy. Heretofore the moral element has been predominant; hereafter the political element receives the chief stress. This is the logical order. Moral decay always precedes political corruption. The lack of high moral standards is the gangrene of any nation. Hosea was particularly adept at tracing the poisonous influence of Israel's sins upon the political life of the nation. He was perhaps the most spiritual of the prophets and at the same time one of the most political. We are indebted to him for a concept of repentance that is unequaled outside the New Testament; yet, he has provided mankind with a criticism of society and politics to which, among the prophets, only Isaiah has added anything. We are in his debt for a concept of God which for the first time in Israel's history challenged idolatry; he was also the first to delineate Israel's position in the political arena of western Asia. With sincerity of conscience Amos courageously announced Israel's destruction because they were evil. To Hosea the insight was given to trace, for example, the effects of moral impurity upon a nation's powers of reproduction as well as upon its intellectual vitality. These two faculties of Hosea are closely associated. To this point he has given the major emphasis to Israel's sins. Now, however, the proportion is reversed and the prophet gives less attention to the sins of his people and more to their consequences in terms of social decay and political folly.

a. Polluted Politics (7:3-7)

This section serves admirably as a transition from Israel's moral defections to an inevitable consequence, corrupt political conditions. Both evils are portrayed in these verses (3-7).

Vital to the interpretation of this section is the identity of the plural subject "they" (v. 3). Some suggest that it points backward to the "bandits" of verse 1. Others hold that it points forward to the plotters or conspirators who throughout the narrative are the subject of the actions described. The latter approach is preferable. These plotters make the king(s) glad with their wickedness and lies. They join with him in carrying out his wicked desires, each in league with the other, but each for himself.

The next four verses (4-7) are admittedly difficult. Most commentators seem to have difficulty with the text, particularly the interpretation of the figure of a baker. In these verses Hosea describes all of them—king, court officials, and conspirators—as adulterers who transgress their relationship with Yahweh by their evil and lies. The plotters burn ("like a heated oven") with passion to consume and destroy. As a baker makes ready the dough, waits overnight for it to rise, then stirs the coals to a blazing flame for baking, so the conspirators devise their plans and wait for the opportune moment to execute them. This moment comes "on the day of our king," either his birthday, anniversary, or some other day in his honor, when he and his officials are "hot" (drunk) from wine (v. 5). The plotters strike with a passion as hot as the oven fire which, banked during the night, is stirred and fed at morning until the flames leap upward.

All are inflamed with the spirit of anarchy, drunkenness, and greed. One king after another falls at the hand of an assassin. The picture is one of moral and political chaos. Polluted politics resulting from polluted participants! It seems certain that Hosea refers to the rapid turnover of kings during the last years of the northern kingdom. Four of her last six kings were murdered (2 Kings 15). This was summons enough for Israel to look beyond herself for help. But none of them cried unto Yahweh; none saw in His righteous rule the security and well-being so avidly sought by all.

b. An Indictment of Ephraim (7:8-16)

Hosea now turns from Ephraim's internal anarchy and political decay to the external affairs. What he sees calls forth his strong denunciation of her faithless foreign policy and her treachery toward Yaweh.

(1) Ephraim's trust in foreign alliances (7:8-12). With reference to Israel's foreign policy Hosea uses two separate analogies to make the comparison. First of all, he compares Israel to a half-baked cake (vv. 8-10). The quest for alliances resulted in a situation in which the nation was neither truly Israelite nor foreign, but half-baked, a "cake not turned," dough on top and burned underneath. As a result the national character was fickle and inconsistent, lacking decisiveness and a sense of direction.

Hosea's second analogy with respect to Israel's foreign policy is that she "is like a dove," silly and without a sense of understanding, "calling to Egypt, going to Assyria" (v. 11). Hosea considered alliances with either Egypt or Assyria as the rejection of Yahweh and he knew that the nation could not escape the consequences of such rejection. In fact, in the very act of their seeking such help instead of returning to God (v. 10), they will land in His net, and He "will bring them down like the birds of the air" (v. 12).

(2) Israel's treachery and unfaithfulness to Yahweh (7:13-16). This oracle begins with a cry of woe, continues by charging the nation with unfaithfulness and treachery to Yahweh (vv. 13-16a), and concludes with a brief note of judgment (v. 16b, c). The theme of the accusation is the incredible treachery of Israel against the God who had been their "help in ages past" and who would have been their "hope for years to come," if only Israel had returned to the One who was truly her redeemer.

It is not surprising that at the very center of the judgment inherent in the word *woe* one finds as its basic cause Baal worship. Although Israel's destruction will result from other factors also—she has "strayed" from the Lord, "rebelled" against His rightful authority, and spoken "lies" against Him—her most heinous sin was "turning to Baal" (vv. 13, 16a). Also involved in Israel's turning from Yahweh was the effort on her part to make use of Canaanite religious practices in an effort to obtain the Lord's favor. This seems to be the meaning of verse 14. Instead of sincerely petitioning Yahweh "from the heart" for grain and wine, "they wail upon their beds [of prayer] and gash themselves" to Yahweh after the manner of the followers of Baal (v. 14; cf. 1 Kings 18:26ff.). The Israelites thought of Yahweh as absent like Baal and sought by various techniques to summon Him to secure His help for their crops. In doing so they stubbornly rebelled against Him.

On Israel's part this was strange action indeed. For had not God's power in past days proved adequate for her to meet the threats and problems of national life? Had not Yahweh "trained and strengthened their arms" (v. 15), enabling Israel to stand before the foe? For Israel to seek strength through alliances with Egypt and Assyria and to turn away from Him to Baal, was to disdain and deny the revelation of God in their history. In turning to Baal Israel was guilty of treachery, like a warped bow that does not shoot straight, whose arrow does not hit the target. Because of this their leaders will become victims of their own folly, for they cannot maintain themselves or their people by the power of the sword. Their death will bring "derision" (v. 16) from the Egyptians whose help they had alternately sought and scorned.

QUESTIONS FOR DISCUSSION

1. Which came first in Israel, political decay and disintegration or moral laxity and corruption? Which is first in any day and age? Does this principle throw some light on the cause

of recent outbreaks of political malpractice
and corruption in America?
2. Do you believe that God has a concern for
the political affairs of a nation? Should
Christians also be concerned? What are some
practical ways of expressing this concern?
3. From Hosea's point of view were foreign alliances a matter of politics or religion? Explain your answer. Does the same hold true
for American foreign policy?

c. False Governments (Kings), Gods, Allies, and Altars (8:1-14)

Chapter 8 begins a new series of oracles. The opening
summons to sound the alarm (v. 1) parallels the beginning of the sequence related to the Syrian-Ephraimite
war in 5:8-14. Here as there a foe is at hand, probably
Assyria. The first oracle (vv. 1-3) not only sets the scene
but also serves to summarize in brief yet comprehensive
fashion the sin and punishment of Israel. The remainder
of the chapter consists of a closely knit sequence of
oracles giving examples of Israel's defection from Yahweh as if to justify the justice of His judgment upon the
nation.

Introduction: Warning of Judgment (8:1-3)

In ancient times the trumpet blast was a sound of
warning given by command of one of high authority (cf.
2 Sam. 2:28; 18:16; 20:22). In this verse (1) the trumpet sounds a clear note of warning to Israel and does so
at the command of the highest authority, Yahweh Himself. Sound the alarm! The enemy is approaching, "a

vulture [eagle] is over the house of the Lord," that is, Israel. The vulture has a fondness for carrion (cf. Job 39:30). Hosea therefore is emphasizing the moral and spiritual decay, the corruption that has flooded the nation. The eagle was also noted for its swiftness (Deut. 28:49). Thus an invader will swiftly pounce upon a decadent and derelict people.

Hosea now sees more doom than hope for Israel. The nation refused to listen, "they have broken my covenant and transgressed my law" (v. 1). The primary breach of the covenant consisted in the substitution of the Canaanite religion for that of Yahweh. God's law has a much wider meaning than a mere code of laws; also included are the teachings, the revelation, and, indeed, the very will of God. This is what Israel had rebelled against or "transgressed." When judgment comes, Israel will cry, "My God, we Israel know thee." But their knowledge is superficial; in reality they do not know Him at all (cf. 4:1; 5:4; 6:6). Note the striking inconsistency: they break the covenant and say, "My God"; rebel against the law and say, "We know you." Yahweh's response is terse and sharp: "Israel has spurned the good; the enemy shall pursue him" (v. 3). The good is everything for which God stands as well as God Himself (cf. Amos 5:4, 6, 14; Mic. 6:8). Israel had forsaken both the good God and the moral good required by His law. Therefore, judgment must take its unalterable course.

The prophet next points out four areas of Israel's life in which she has proven false to Yahweh, thereby making His judgment certain. They are: false governments, gods, allies, and altars.

(1) False governments (8:4). The setting up of kings may go back as far as the early establishment of the monarchy (1 Sam. 8:4-7). To say the least, this initial arrangement was not pleasing to God. It may also have reference to the division of the kingdom at Solomon's

death. For while God was involved in the selection of Jeroboam I as king of Israel, the division itself was the result of sin, and therefore contrary to God's choosing. The northern kingdom of Israel had known eighteen kings represented by ten different dynasties, each of which came to a violent end. During the final years of the kingdom there were frequent assassinations. The charismatic selection of kings had given way to intrigue and power politics in which were contained the seeds of strife and corruption. In the sense, then, that the kings had been selected by men rather than God they were false kings.

The last part of this verse probably refers to the bulls which Jeroboam I set up at Dan and Bethel (1 Kings 12:28ff.). Hosea thus puts idol and king on the same level of falsity—both were made by Israel, the mark of their rebellion against Yahweh. It is noteworthy that Hosea was the first prophet to denounce the use of images in worship, and this passage contains the first denunciation of the bulls which Jeroboam set up. The closing line of the verse seems somewhat paradoxical. Did the people make idols for the nation's destruction? Of course they did not intend it so when making them, but since this was the inevitable result of their manufacture, Hosea identifies the result with the people's intent in making them.

(2) False gods (8:5-7). These verses continue the subject of idols and idolatry suggested in verse 4 and are concerned with the particular theme of Samaria's bull image. This oracle proclaims Yahweh's attitude and future action toward one of Israel's most famous images. "Samaria" refers either to the land or to the residents of the capital city, not to the city itself since it is doubtful whether a bull image was ever set up in Samaria. The Israelites probably never used this image as an idol to be worshiped, but rather as a pedestal or throne for Yah-

weh who is invisible. (Some insist that verse 6 indicates otherwise.) Though the image had been set up as an aid to Yahweh worship, it was associated with the Baal cult of Canaan and its use, however noble, was certain to result in confusion, syncretism, and outright idolatry. Yahweh's response to any use made of the bull was the same as it was to the image made at Sinai (Exod. 32:10f.). His burning anger (v. 5) is always against those who turn to other gods (cf. Num. 25:3; Josh. 23:16), thus breaking a covenantal regulation (Exod. 20:3f.). The last line of this verse, "How long . . . they are pure," an interrogatory exclamation, is in reality a cry of anguish and sorrow over Israel's failure to live free of guilt and deeds that prevent her from knowing Yahweh. This points in peculiar fashion to Israel's idolatry. In this close proximity of lament and burning wrath, Hosea's God discloses something of the suffering in which His election of Israel had involved Him. His wrath is not a bitter hatred, but the determined passion of a purpose (for Israel) that will not despair in spite of frustration and repeated rejection.

Verse 6 states the reason for Yahweh's rejection of the calf of Samaria. It had come from the hands of man. It was the product of human creation, and, as such, it was not God nor could it represent Him. It was a false god. Therefore, broken in pieces, it will be able to deliver neither itself nor the people.

A further declaration of Israel's destruction is indicated in verse 7 which contains both the theme and climax of chapter 8. It is difficult to determine whether this verse is related to Israel's folly in seeking help from Samaria's calf (vv. 5-6) or to her futile international policy (vv. 8-10). Fortunately it matters little since the general principle of the proverbial sayings is equally applicable.

The consequences of Israel's conduct are described by two figures taken from the harvest field. The first, "they sow the wind and . . . reap the whirlwind," is a figure frequently used to illustrate the divine law of retribution (cf. Hos. 10:13; 12:2; Job. 4:8; Gal. 6:7). With these words Hosea was declaring the world a moral universe in which judgment is an inevitable consequence of sin. It is impossible to escape the consequence of one's own actions. In worshiping the calf and courting other nations, Israel has sown that which is "illusive and elusive" (wind) and so shall reap a harvest of destruction (whirlwind).

In the second figure of verse 7 the standing grain has no heads; it has failed to develop. Therefore it will produce no meal. Or as another has said, "Grain without growth [development] yields no meal."[4] Israel's dependence on the cult for fertility and her reliance on the nations for security will be of no avail. And if some grain should be produced, invading strangers ("aliens") would consume it.

(3) False allies (8:8-10). Israel's appeals to the nations will prove futile. Already she is being "swallowed up" among the nations. Everything distinctive in her way of life is gone. She is "as a useless vessel" (v. 8), without influence or status. They have gone to Assyria seeking assistance (v. 9). Like the wild ass, the most stupid of animals, which stubbornly leaves the herd (with which it usually runs) to seek its own willfull way, Israel, just as stubbornly, seeks her security and freedom in alliances with the nations. In a further attempt to obtain favorable alliances "Ephraim has hired lovers." Here Israel is pictured as a harlot, little sought and frantic for lovers, who gives away her favors as gifts.

Though Israel prostitutes herself in such fashion, it will not avail. Yahweh will gather her from among the

---

4. James L. Mays, *Hosea* (Philadelphia: The Westminster Press, 1969), p. 120.

nations and in judgment carry her to Assyria where there will be a cessation from a constant anointing of godless kings and princes (v. 10). The last half of this verse is difficult. The King James Version reads: "They shall sorrow a little for the burden of the king of princes" ("king of princes" refers to the Assyrian king).

(4) False altars (8:11-14). These verses provide additional justification for the threat of exile in verse 10. It was a popular notion of Hosea's day that building altars was a pious act, since this meant more sacrifice and sacrifice atoned for whatever sins were committed. Yet Hosea has no commendation for the people for their building of many altars. His startling word to them is that the many altars built to deal with sin have actually become a place to sin (v. 11). This is certainly no denunciation of the sacrificial system as such. Rather it denounces the people's use of it as part of their ritualistic worship. Sacrifice had become an end within itself (cf. Amos 4:4f.), and certain Canaanitish practices associated with it were occasions for sensuous evil (4:13f.). So, just as the expansion of the priesthood meant an increase in iniquity (4:7), the increase in the number of altars resulted in an increase in sinning.

Verse 12 continues the prophet's condemnation of sacrifices (altars) as engaged in by the people. If the laws of God already written were increased to ten thousand, they would be of no more weight in Israel's eyes than if they were laws of a foreign country. Thus Hosea condemns priest and people for forgetting Yahweh and His moral requirements while they were zealously attending to every detail of their sacrificial worship.

Israel disregards God's law (v. 12) because they hold that their relations with Him are best established and continued by means of the sacrificial cult. This was true because "they love sacrifice; they sacrifice flesh and eat it" (v. 13). Sacrificing, then, did not draw them closer to

God. It was performed for selfish reasons, was often a mere formality used as an excuse for indulging in the luxury of eating meat. But this worship was so displeasing to God that He will "now" punish their iniquity, "They shall return to Egypt." "Egypt" here probably stands for bondage; the prophet hardly means they will literally return to Egypt but will be carried to bondage in Assyria. By comparing this verse with 9:3 and 11:5 some commentators have suggested that the meaning is that when Assyria overruns Israel the populace will either have to submit to deportation to Assyria or flee as refugees to Egypt.

In verse 14 the sin of Israel is once again traced to its source, "For Israel has forgotten his Maker." The nation's false or misplaced trust in government (kings), gods, allies, and altars has claimed the prophet's attention to this point in the chapter. Now, as if to give one more example of such trust, Hosea charges Israel (and Judah) with a false trust in fortifications (palaces and fortresses) for her security. But such man-made feats can result only in a false sense of security. God will send a destructive fire and these objects of national trust and confidence will become the ashes of a misdirected and false faith.

d. From Mirth to Mourning—Exile (9:1-9)

The repeated, brief warnings of judgment in chapter 8 (vv. 1-3, 7, 10b, 13c, 14c) are here joined in an expanded oracle portraying Israel's exile, when the mirth of her "religious" festivals will be changed to mourning. The Israelites celebrated three major feasts during the year, all connected in some way to harvest time. At Easter there was the Passover when the first of the ripened grains of barley were offered to the Lord. Seven weeks later the Feast of Pentecost was observed in conjunction with the wheat harvest. At summer's end came the Feast of Tabernacles in association with the grape harvest. It was probably at this festive occasion, when wine flowed like water, that Hosea stepped forth and warned the assembled worshipers that this festival would be their last; their crops will fail them and they themselves will be carried into an unclean land where the worship of Yahweh is impossible. The sanctuary where they are now assembled will lie abandoned, covered with weeds instead of worshipers. Mirth will indeed be replaced with mourning!

(1) Fasting instead of feasting (9:1-6). Rejoicing and celebration were a common feature of the autumn festival held at the conclusion of the harvest season. Though the feast in progress was held in the name of Yahweh (cf. vv. 4f.), Hosea viewed it as another expression of Israel's apostasy. The people were making material gain the reward of worship, a gift from the gods of the land. They had departed from Yahweh and now were accepting the bountiful harvest as a harlot's hire for their spiritual prostitution before the Baals of the land (v. 1). But this bounty will fail (v. 2); exile is on its way. Israel will no longer dwell in "Jehovah's land" (v. 3). Those who do not return to God will return to Egypt and go to Assyria.

In exile the cult will end; no more wine-offerings poured out to Yahweh, no more sacrifices of joy to Him. All those will have ceased and their bread, now contaminated, will not be eaten in sweet communion with Yahweh, but only for physical satisfaction (v. 4). Those who for so long sought only physical benefits from their worship will have their desire satisfied, only to find that man cannot live by bread alone (Deut. 8:3). "What will you [Israel] do" (v. 5) when the time comes for festive occasions to honor Yahweh? How will you then celebrate the harvest festivals? Yahweh's judgment will have ended their worship of Him. What will they do? The question is left unanswered and the silence created is the beginning of the end of all their festivities.

In verse 6 Hosea returns to the threatened judgment of Yahweh now about to engulf His people. The first line of this verse reads more literally, "For behold, they are going *from destruction*," rather than *"to Assyria."* That is, when destruction ravages the land, those who can, will escape to Egypt. But they will find no future there beyond a gathering for burial in the famous ancient graveyards of Memphis. The nation to which they had so often turned, seeking an escape from Assyria, will prove finally to be the instrument of their humiliation. The shrine that is now so full of celebrants will be deserted, abandoned to wind and weeds. And Israel's prized possessions—idols, heirlooms, cult objects, even houses—will be overrun with "nettles" and "thorns."

(2) Rejection instead of repentance (9:7-9). When Hosea declared that "the days of punishment . . . [and] recompense have come" (v. 7a), the populace turned on him with the scornful accusation, "The prophet is a fool, the man of the spirit is mad." In these words there is found a commentary on the response to the prophet's message, the only such appraisal in the entire book. The Hebrew word for "fool" used here describes one who is obstinately stupid. In some of its uses it carries the suggestion of licentiousness.[5] Could it be that Hosea was subtly linked with the adulterous activities of his wife? Also in the terminology "man of the spirit" there may lie a note of contempt, since the Hebrew word for "spirit" also means "wind." Jeremiah later calls attention to the practice of referring to prophets as "windbags" (Jer. 5:13).

---

5. Jacob M. Myers, "The Book of Hosea," *The Layman's Bible Commentary* (Richmond: John Knox Press, 1959), p. 48.

Hosea answers their charge by pointing to its real cause, "your great iniquity and great hatred," that is, their iniquitous practices in their worship and their hatred toward the prophet for his reminding them of it. Furthermore the true prophet was the watchman for his people, warning them of danger (Ezek. 3:17; Jer. 7:17ff.). This Hosea was seeking to do. But Israel, instead of showing gratitude for his work, sought to ensnare and trap him as if he were no better than a wild animal, and showed their hatred of him even unto the very house of God (v. 8).

As Hosea looked for an experience in the history of his people with which to compare the depth of their current corruption, he points to the action of their fathers at Gibeah, when one of the tribes was all but wiped out because of its wickedness (Judg. 19–21). A similar depravity on Israel's part will inevitably result in equal retribution.

This section on God's judgment upon Israel (9:1-9) concludes a larger division (7:3–9:9) which deals with the nation's unfaithfulness and political instability resulting from her moral decay (4:4–7:2). In this larger division it has become evident that the spirit of national unity had largely disappeared. Society was as a "cake not turned," half-baked, raw on one side and burned on the other. The nation was broken into factions and produced no king with God's hand upon him to lead it. Monarchs were man-made and as quickly murdered; anarchy reigned supreme. Surrounding nations held Israel in contempt even as they exhausted her strength through alliances favorable to themselves. Though Israel's need is to "return to their God," Hosea sees this as impossible as far as the nation is concerned. Furthermore, he is convinced that her deep-seated corruption is no recent phenomenon. So he turns to probe deeper into the nation's history seeking for the roots which have produced the fruits of national depravity and decay.

1. In this section Hosea points out four objects in which Israel's vain (false) hopes are centered. What are they? (For help see especially 8:4, 5-7, 8-10, 11-14.)
2. Wherein lay the strong appeal of Baal worship to Israel? Were the immoral practices associated with this worship based solely on sexual desires? (A knowledge of the hoped for, utilitarian values of these practices in terms of increased productivity of soil, cattle, and man will enable one to better understand their strong attraction upon the Israelites. This in no way condones such practices.)
3. In the larger section dealing with the Lord's controversy with His people (4:1—9:9), what are some of the charges brought against them? (See especially chapters 4—6.) Might similar charges justly be brought against America? Give examples. When a nation is guilty of such charges, can it expect other than judgment as indicated by the prophet in 9:1-9?

B. Historical Retrospect and Israel's Current Crisis (9:10—12:14)

At this point in Hosea's prophecies there is a definite break in the literary structure which makes for a clear-cut division between 9:9 and 9:10. Prior to this division few historical references are found. Following the division repeated reference is made to past events in the nation's history. The continuing moral decay and political disintegration of Israelitish society caused the prophet to turn more and more to past history in his search for the fountainhead of Israel's current infidelity to Yahweh. The depth of his nation's depravity was such that it could not have occurred in a moment; its roots went deep into her past. So, in a series of events related to successive sites in Israel's past history, Hosea discovers the wellsprings of national whoredom. It is obvious that the prophet is in nowise seeking to clear his own generation of the guilt of their apostasy. Rather, his purpose is to show that Israel's current corruption is inseparably related to a larger break of covenant relationship and law which has characterized the nation's history from its beginning.

1. Israel's Ancient Apostasy (9:10-17)

The prophet's point is crystal clear: Israel's current apostasy is no recent thing. It dates back even before her entrance into the land, and succeeding events only served to show that this apostasy was deeply entrenched in the nation's character.

a. Apostasy at Baal-peor (9:10-14)

In this section the striking contrast between *then* and *now* is delineated. It opens with the description of Yahweh's delight in His choice of Israel to be His people. He looked upon them with the pleasure of a weary and hungry traveler in the wilderness who chances upon a vine loaded with grapes or with the joy of the gardener over the first ripe figs of the season (v. 10). But at Baal-peor Israel had corrupted herself (see Num. 25:1-9). The very people to whom God has shown so much love set themselves apart in ritual consecration to a deity whom they thought would create fertility for them in the land they were about to enter. Baal-peor, then, stood for apostasy and harlotry into which the people fell in Moab. This defection is not described as a temporary lapse on Israel's part, but as a definite attitude of determined commitment: they "consecrated themselves to Baal, and became detestable like the thing they loved" (v. 10).

As Israel had suffered punishment when first she went "a whoring" after other gods, she will also feel the hand of God's judgment in her latest disloyalty to Him— "Ephraim's glory shall fly away like a bird" (v. 11). Israel's glory was her children in whom she saw her future strength and the evidence of God's blessings. The most terrible calamity that could befall the nation would be "no birth, no pregnancy, no conception"—their extinction as a people. But now the prospect is that Israel will be cut off, for "even if they bring up children, I will bereave them till none is left" (v. 12), and "Ephraim's sons . . . are destined for a prey" (v. 13).

In light of the horrors to come upon his people, Hosea prayed that God might give them "a miscarrying womb and dry breasts" (v. 14). God's judgments are always just and right, so the prophet prays that the children may be cut off before they are born that they may be spared these countless horrors. The consequences of Baal-peor will be as disastrous for Israel now as they were in the early days of her history.

b. Apostasy at Gilgal (9:15-17)

These verses are closely related to the previous section (vv. 10-14). The plural pronouns of verse 15 have as their antecedent "Ephraim" of verses 11 and 13. And verse 16 returns to the theme of infertility and the death of Ephraim's children as if to emphasize the punishments already announced (vv. 11-13).

The first line of verse 15 can be translated in either past or present tense. Reference to Baal-peor (9:10) and

Gibeah (9:9, 10:9) favors the past tense; hence the prophet refers to some incident at Gilgal in Israel's history when she was guilty of sin for which she must now pay the price of God's judgment. Gilgal was the place of an early sanctuary and as such had received condemnation from more than one of the prophets (see Amos 4:4, 5:5; Hos. 4:15, 12:11). Also the first king of united Israel, Saul, was anointed there (1 Sam. 11:14f.), an act in violation of the covenant which had recognized Yahweh alone as king. Perhaps Hosea proposed that the two besetting sins of Israel, Baal worship and trust in humanly appointed kings, had an ancient origin. Israel craved a human king, visible and present, as well as a visible present God. All their wickedness in calf and king, in apostasy and disloyalty is associated with Gilgal. It was "there I began to hate them," the Lord says. This is surely not hate in the common meaning of the word, for God hates no man. Hosea uses the statement to express the depth of God's threat against Israel and the extent to which the covenant relationship had been fractured. And "because of the wickedness of their deed" Yahweh will drive them out of the land ("my house"). As Adam and Eve were driven from Eden (Gen. 3:24) when their sin separated them from God, so Israel shall be separated from their land as the result of their sins.

In verse 16 a previous thought is resumed; fruitful Ephraim has become fruitless (cf. vv. 11-12). Israel is like a plant whose leaves fall because its roots fail to find moisture. Such a plant can produce no fruit. Even if Ephraim brings forth, her "beloved children" will be slain in war. And because the nation cast off Yahweh at Gilgal "my God will cast them off" (v. 17). Since Israel has strayed from Yahweh and has rebelled against Him (see 7:13), they can no longer expect Him to be their God ("my God"). The curse of Cain (Gen. 4:12ff.) will be upon them, "they shall be wanderers among the nations." While this threat clearly suggests exile for Israel, more is implied. As Cain was condemned to be a fugitive and a wanderer, so Israel will be estranged and homeless, alone among the nations and lacking that fellowship with God without which life is meaningless.

2. Yahweh's Judgment on False Gods and Kings (10:1-8)

To this point Hosea has charged Israel with the twin sins of trust in idols (Baal-worship) and trust in human kings rather than in God as king. He has shown that the nation's deep-seated defection in both of these areas is of long standing and will result in God's judgment (see 9:10-17). In this section (10:1-8) the prophet comes to deal more specifically with this judgment—one which will result in the loss of both cult and king.

In another of his numerous metaphors Hosea pictures an Israel that has prospered, but in her success has come to failure. She is described as a luxuriant vine that puts forth its shoots and bears abundant fruit (v. 1). She should have proved pleasing to Yahweh since it was He who gave her the increase; instead the nation multiplied altars and improved worship centers to Baal. The more the land produced, the more altars were built. Altars and pillars were the "holy machinery which produced the prosperity," so the people thought. The altars therefore had "become to him [Israel] . . . for sinning" (8:11).

Israel's sin is centered in the charge, "Their heart is false" (v. 2). For the Hebrews the "heart" was not so much the center of emotions as the seat of will and intellect, and the center of volitional decisions. Israel's problem, then, was one of the will, of volitional decision and commitment. Who has Israel's devotion, Yahweh or Baal? Because of her divided ("false") heart, "now they must bear their guilt," part of which punishment will be the destruction of altars and pillars so dear to them.

In verse 3 Hosea returns to his theme of the kingship

and its failure. As with the multiplication of altars, the prophet views the nation's misplaced trust in man-made kings as resulting from the divided heart (cf. "now," vv. 2, 3). And because Israel's heart is divided she will experience the overthrow of throne as well as altar. Hosea foresees a time of judgment when Israel has no king because they do not fear the Lord. In such a time, "a king, what could he do for us?" The answer to this disillusioned question is poured out in embittered phrases which summarize Israel's experience with their kings. They only speak empty words of allegiance to the Lord and swear falsely in making covenants they do not intend to keep. And their judgments, bitter and deadly to the wronged, are as numerous as the poisonous weeds of the field (v. 4).

In verse 5 Hosea returns to the theme of Israel's cult and deals specifically with the "detestable" object which stood at its very center, the bull of Beth-aven. This verse is replete with ironic indignation at the coming collapse of Israel's idolatry. "The inhabitants of Samaria tremble" for their golden calf. Instead of saving them, the calf becomes a source of anxiety to them—how can they save it? In the face of impending judgment people and priests mourn for its safety (and theirs). An ever-present and pertinent question is raised: How powerful is your god? In the crises of life is it necessary to carry him, or is he abundantly able to bear you (cf. Isa. 46:1-4)?

What can be so humiliating to a people as to have the god in whom they trust and whom they worship carried away captive? This will now happen to Israel. The god to which she brought offerings and rich gifts as tribute will in turn be offered as tribute to a greater and more powerful god, the king of Assyria (v. 6). The calf at Beth-aven (Bethel) is unable to save itself. How can it save its worshipers? Israel will learn at last the futility and shame of setting up a dumb idol (calf) as protector of the nation.

The reference in verse 7 to "Samaria's king" has been taken two ways. Some consider the king as a reference to the calf of Beth-aven (vv. 5f.). The fact that verse 7 is set within the context of sayings about the cult lends support to this view. Others view "Samaria's king" as referring to the actual king of Samaria. This interpretation seems the more likely not only because of Hosea's antagonism toward the kingship in Israel (cf. 8:4, 10; 13:10f.), but also because of his fondness for denouncing simultaneously the twin sins of Israel, man-made gods and man-made kings (see v. 10b and comment on 9:15a). The king of Samaria (Israel) is as helpless as a chip of wood carried along by swollen flood waters. The destruction of the monarchy indicated here is nothing less than the destruction of the nation by the enemy.

"The high places of Aven" (Beth-aven, or Bethel) are doomed for destruction, because they are "the sin of Israel" (v. 8). Since the high places (worship centers) are the source of Israel's wickedness, they will fall into disuse and thorns and thistles will cover them. Then the people, left without god or king, will cry out in shame and terror for the mountains and hills to erupt and cover them that they not be left in their nakedness to face the wrath of a righteous God.

3. Israel's Ancient Apostasy at Gibeah (10:9-10)

In order to reemphasize the deeply engrained character of Israel's iniquity, Hosea again links the character of her present predicament with sin committed at an ancient site (cf. 9:10, 15). "From the days of Gibeah, you have sinned, O Israel" (v. 9). The occasion of Israel's sin at Gibeah is not clear. The reference may be to the brutal assault of the Levite's concubine at Gibeah (Judg. 19), and the subsequent civil war in which the tribe of Benjamin was all but exterminated (Judg. 20–21). If this is the reference, then the prophet's point is that from the very beginning Israel has been guilty of both a breach of covenant morality, shown in the assault of the Levite's concubine, and civil war in the extreme revenge taken on Benjamin.

Others find in this reference to Gibeah the suggestion that Israel's present predicament actually originated with the initiation of kingship under Saul. (Gibeah was Saul's place of residence during his kingship [see 1 Sam. 10:26; 11:14].) In this view kingship on Israel's part was an effort to guarantee her future apart from God. As such its establishment was evidence of a lack of faith in, if not outright repudiation of, the sole leadership of Yahweh. As a matter of fact, both historical events may be in the mind of the prophet. In either case what happened there continued to the present. Gibeah had become a site in the spiritual geography of Israel. "There" designates a way of life which Israel was still pursuing. Therefore war will "overtake them in Gibeah." Yahweh will "chastise" (discipline; see comment on 5:2) His "wayward people" through the "nations" whom He will assemble against them because of "their double iniquity" (v. 10). Though some consider the two events occurring at Gibeah as discussed above the source of the "double iniquity" of Israel, more probably the two transgressions are man-made gods and man-made kings, both of which were basically a rejection of Yahweh as their God and king.

4. WORDS of Woe—a WORD of Hope (10:11-13a)

Using figures drawn from farm life, Hosea warns of difficult days ahead for Israel. In the wilderness Ephraim was treated gently by Yahweh as she was responsive to His guidance and direction. Ephraim was a trained heifer that "loved to thresh," and Yahweh "spared her fair neck" (v. 11). The treading of the grain was an easy task, offering the ox all the grain it desired (see Deut. 25:4) and involving no yoke. Thus Ephraim was favored when obedient to her owner. But Ephraim changed from Yahweh to the Baals, and a grievous change awaits her. More strenuous work is in store: yoking, plowing, harrowing. On her unscarred neck Yahweh will place a yoke preparatory to the hard work of the plow. Plowing and harrowing are symbols of God's judgment on Israel now imminent on the national horizon. In the days to come things will be different for her. The bondage of exile will present a decided contrast to blessings which previously were so carelessly enjoyed at the provident hand of God.

Verse 12, coming as it does between verses 11 and 13, is like "a ray of sunlight through a cloudy sky." Verse 11 describes the heavy yoke that Israel's sin has brought upon her, while verse 13 amplifies and elaborates the tragic results of the nation's continued disobedience. In between there is found a word of hope and comfort, a warm and winsome appeal to return to Yahweh before it is too late. For the last time, perhaps, the Lord exhorts His people to sow such seeds (of "righteousness") as shall enable them to harvest the "fruit of steadfast love." If prior to her sowing Israel will "break up [her] fallow ground," that is, break up the old habits, leave off traveling the old road, turn in a new direction, and sincerely seek the Lord, then He will indeed "come and rain salvation [deliverance] upon [her]" (v. 12).

Rejection of the prophet's exhortation (v. 12) is evident. In fact, Israel's actions were in direct opposition to the exhortation. Instead of sowing righteousness, Israel "plowed iniquity"; and instead of reaping the fruit of steadfast love, she "reaped injustice" (v. 13a). This resulted in her utter disappointment: "You have eaten the fruit of lies." The word for "lies" means that which deceives, disappoints, or fails one. Israel's plowing and reaping resulted only in disappointing failure.

5. The Fruit of False Trust—War (10:13b-15)

Israel's trust in "warriors" and "chariots" (v. 13b) will end in disaster for the nation. The very objects of her trust will be turned upon her and all of her "fortresses shall be destroyed" (v. 14). Israel's agony in such a crisis will be comparable to that experienced when "Shalman destroyed Beth-arbel" and "mothers were dashed in pieces with their children." The reference to a battle of Beth-arbel is obscure. It is not known whether Shalman was an Assyrian king (Shalmaneser) or the Shalaman of Moab mentioned in an inscription of Tiglath-pileser III; nor is it known which Beth-arbel is designated. Nevertheless the event was fresh in the mind of people and prophet and was used to illustrate the calamity that befalls nations who trust in human resources. Application is made to Israel in verse 15. Because of Israel's "great wickedness" her king will be suddenly and utterly cut off.

QUESTIONS FOR DISCUSSION

1. Prior to 9:6 Hosea makes but scant reference to past events in Israel's history. From this point on (through chapter 12), however, repeated reference is made to such events. What is the prophet's purpose in such references? Is it to clear his own generation of any guilt for its current apostasy, or to magnify the protracted and deep-seated character of national whoredom?

2. Hosea denounces false gods on numerous occasions. What is a false god? Is idol worship the only example of the worship of a false god? Explain your answer. Name some false gods America is guilty of worshiping.

---

6. Egypt: Antecedents to Israel's Current Apostasy (11:1-11)

In this chapter Hosea continues his motif of historical retrospection as a literary device for illustrating the character of Israel's relationship with Yahweh. On three previous occasions in chapters 4–14 (9:10, 15; 10:9) he had gone back to Israel's early history for the purpose of emphasizing some current defect in the nation's character. Here (chap. 11) appeal is made to the history of Israel not only to point out a long-time defect in national character, but also to give emphasis to an aspect of God's character (His love), in light of which Israel's sin is all the blacker and more deserving of punishment.

Chapter 11 has been fittingly described as "one of the greatest chapters in the Bible." It contains some of the most compassionate and tender verses in the entire book, and certainly nowhere else in the Old Testament is the depth of God's love so vividly, yet pathetically portrayed.

a. The Fatherhood of God (11:1-7)

The reader is already familiar with Hosea's use of the figure of husband and wife to describe the relationship of God to His people. Here he makes use of a second metaphor from family life, the father-son relationship. "When Israel was a child, I loved him, and out of Egypt I called my son" (v. 1). "Called" is an election term and describes that experience in the nation's life when Yahweh called them from bondage in Egypt into a covenant relationship which Hosea interprets from the family perspective of love, sonship, and faithfulness. The sole basis of Israel's call was God's love, a love which moved Him to choose Israel to be His adopted son and thus to share in His bountiful blessing, if obedient to Him.

The figure (father-son) is continued in verse 3a: "I taught Ephraim to walk . . . took them up in my arms."

As a loving father, Yahweh had taken the infant Israel by the arms and carefully supported him as he took his first steps. When Ephraim fell, it was Yahweh who tenderly lifted him in His mighty arms and healed his hurt.

Numerous interpreters hold that in verse 4b (perhaps v. 4a) the figure changes from the father's care of a child to the driver's care for his beast (ox). When the heavy yoke chafed the animal's neck, the compassionate driver went to its head and moved the yoke to give the ox a period of relief during which it could eat. Thus the figure is illustrative of God's concern for Israel. Since a second figure seems to break the chain of thought relative to the fatherhood of God in verses 1-4, it has been suggested that the same figure be continued through verse 4. This can be accomplished by the change of a single vowel in the Hebrew text ("o" to "u"), making "yoke" read "infant" as follows: "I became to them as one who lifts an infant to his cheeks."[6] However, either figure speaks of God's compassionate and tender concern for His child (Ephraim).

But what was Israel's response to Yahweh's calling and fatherly care? Hosea, speaking for Yahweh, charged, "The more I called them, the more they went from me" (v. 2). The first clause is a vivid expression of the persistence of God's love that will not let His people go; the second is an equally terse statement of the nation's persistent apostasy. The more God sent His prophets to warn and call the people to Himself, the more "they kept sacrificing to the Baals, and burning incense to idols" (v. 2). Though Yahweh like a father taught Israel to walk and carefully watched every stumble, yet Israel showed no discernment, she did not realize that Yahweh was her protector. She took His blessings for granted, ascribing them to Baal. Since she has spurned the guid-

---

6. Roy L. Honeycutt, "Hosea," pp. 49f.

ance and care of her Father, she must now undergo the discipline that a loving father cannot withhold.

With verse 5 there is a sudden change of tone in Hosea's message. Tender words of loving care are terminated and punishment is threatened. An enemy will come and punish the wayward son, stubbornly intent on turning away from Yahweh (v. 7). The bondage from which Israel was originally delivered will be restored. The "Egypt" of their bondage will be Assyria. The one whom they had trusted for deliverance will place a yoke upon their neck, for "Assyria shall be their king" (v. 5). Their cities will be ravished with the sword and their fortified places overthrown (v. 6). The yoke which was lifted from the ox (v. 4) to allow it to eat will now become a fixture on its (Ephraim's) neck. Nothing can save the nation from the yoke which they, because of their determination to follow their own way, are about to impose upon themselves.

b. The Divine Dilemma (11:8-11)

The threat of judgment and captivity (vv. 5-7) is followed by one of the most moving passages in the entire book. Its theme is the theme of Hosea, namely, the mercy and unmerited love of God. In these verses (8-9) the unwearied love of God breaks forth in rich tenderness and unparalleled beauty.

Though Israel has forsaken Yahweh, we hear Him cry out in deep agony of soul, "How can I give you up, O Ephraim. . . . How can I make you like Admah . . . like Zeboiim!" This heartrending cry expresses the undying love of a parent for a child; however unworthy the child, the father will never cease, yea, cannot cease loving him. The struggle within the very heart of God is intense; justice demands one thing, but mercy and love temper its demands. "My heart recoils within me" speaks of an emotional upheaval, a turmoil of feelings. Justice and mercy strive together. God's holiness and righteousness demand that stubborn and unfaithful Israel be punished, but punishment does not mean that God has ceased to love. God *is* love, and if He were to cease to love He would cease to be God. His disposition to love is both constant and indestructible. How, then, can He destroy Israel as He destroyed Admah and Zeboiim with Sodom and Gomorrah (cf. Gen. 14:2, 8-12; 19:24-29; Deut. 29:23)? He cannot! "I will not execute my fierce anger" (v. 9). His love transcends His righteous judgments. He is not bound by the demands of the covenant to annihilate the faithless partner. Because of the depth of His love He exceeds the limits of covenant obligation, and acts toward Israel in the realm of pure grace (unmerited favor). How did God do this? The answer is found in God's own words, "I am God and not man." Contrary to man, there is found with God that perfect union of love and grace which makes it possible for Him not only to forgive but to discipline and to recreate. This He did with Israel and continues to do with His people in every age, individually and collectively.

This deep and forgiving love of God does not remove the penalties of His judgments upon man; these are inescapable. However, it does say to man that God's judgments, since they are controlled by love, are redemptive and disciplinary rather than punitive and destructive. This fact is illustrated in the next verses (10-11), for love's victory is assured as Israel responds to the discipline of an exile with loving obedience as Yahweh loudly ("roar like a lion") but lovingly calls them back home.

7. Patriarchal Antecedents: Lessons from the Past (11:12–12:14)

In this section Hosea continues his motif (theme) of historical retrospection as the key to an understanding of Israel's current crisis (cf. 9:10, 15; 10:9). Here, however, instead of looking to ancient sites and events for the sole purpose of showing the early and continuing character of Israel's sin (cf. 9:10, 15; 10:9), he presents episodes in the life of a patriarchal ancestor, Jacob, for the purpose of exhorting Israel to comparable action.

a. Reiteration of Israel's Guilt (11:12–12:1)

In characteristic fashion Hosea now abruptly turns from Israel's salvation (deliverance) to her sin. Yahweh speaks and charges the nation with so surrounding Him with lies and deceit that He can see nothing else (11:12). In contrast, Judah is faithful to the Holy One and consequently is still known by Him. Some question the genuineness of this and all other references to Judah in Hosea. Others feel that the last half of the verse should parallel the first; therefore Judah must be condemned as is Israel. The marginal reading in the American Standard Version gives this sense: "And Judah is yet unstedfast with God, and with the Holy One who is faithful."

The nature of Ephraim's deception and falsehood is indicated in the statement "They make a bargain with Assyria, and oil is carried to Egypt" (12:1b). This is usually associated with Israel's deception in her efforts to court both Assyria and Egypt; while she is in the process of making a covenant with the one, she is courting the other. But a more serious charge is made. Israel had entered into covenant with Yahweh. For her to enter into covenant with any other was the height of her betrayal of Yahweh. This she had done, for Hosea uses the familiar expression to "cut a covenant" in describing Israel's "bargain" with Assyria. The parallel expression "and oil is carried to Egypt" also suggests that a covenant was made with Egypt. Rather than seeking the Lord and striving to live up to their covenant with Him Israel is playing the game of international politics and intrigue. Such action on her part is as futile and foolish as would be the efforts of a shepherd to tend the wind rather than the flocks, or a hunter who hunts not game but the deadly and destructive "east wind" (*sirocco*).

b. Jacob: Accusation and Commendation (12:2-6)

The lawsuit motif introduces verses 2-6 (see comments on 4:1-3), a lawsuit involving both ancient and modern Jacob. (It is highly probable that "Judah" has been substituted for an original "Israel" in v. 2a.) A basic part of this type of prophetic speech is the accusation or charge brought against the accused, in this case Jacob (Israel). In the previous section (11:12–12:1) Israel was charged with falsehood and deceit. Now, as if to show that this was a deep-seated tendency which had been present from the beginning in their ancestor Jacob, Hosea makes use of history to prove his case. In verses 3-5 he refers to experiences in the early life of Israel's patriarchal forebear which gave emphasis to his practice of deception and trickery (see Gen. 25:19-34; 27).

These same verses (3-5) also refer to incidents in the life of Jacob which are commendable and in which Hosea points to him as an example of one who had power with God (see Gen. 32; 35:1-15). Reference to the history of the patriarch Jacob serves, then, as a warning and as an exhortation (to Israel). It warned the nation of the deep-rooted nature of its love for lies and its dealings in deceit, and of the necessity to cease from such betrayal of their covenant relationship with Yahweh. At the same time it was an exhortation to the nation as Hosea pointed to Jacob as one who through weeping and supplication found strength and favor with God. The power of Jacob to prevail was the power for Israel if they would return to God, demonstrate love and justice to their fellowmen, "and wait continually for your God" (v. 6). To "wait for Him" is to trust Him and to allow Him to lead the way. This Israel must do; it is her only salvation.

c. Ephraim: Israelite or Canaanite (12:7-14)?

In the previous section (12:2-6) Israel's esteemed and
venerable ancestor Jacob is commended for his return to
Yahweh after a life of deception and guile, and Israel is
exhorted to follow his example in returning to God. But
instead of following the example of Jacob, who in a
struggle with God prevailed and was given a new name
(Israel) indicative of a change in character, Ephraim had
become a "trader" (more literally, *Canaan* or *Canaanite*).
Since the Canaanites were a merchant people, "trader"
and "Canaanite" were synonymous terms, and both were
a derisive and scornful characterization of Ephraim. Not
an Israelite but a Canaanite—a trickster with false bal-
ances in his hands (v. 8)! Though Ephraim is practicing
deceit in obtaining wealth, he boasts that he has no sin
against him. The Lord then warns Ephraim that he is not
dealing with man, but with Yahweh who knows all
about him, since He had delivered him from Egypt. And
because of Ephraim's corrupt practices, Yahweh will
drive them out of their land, and they will dwell in tents
as they did in the wilderness and on the days of the
commemorative Feast of Tabernacles (v. 9). The Lord
who gave the land can take it back, along with all the
wealth of which Ephraim boasted. Furthermore, Yahweh has made known His purposes through the "prophets" to whom He gave "visions" and "parables" (v. 10).
Consequently, any "iniquity in Gilead . . . shall surely
come to nought," and because of the sacrifices at Gilgal
its altars will become as heaps of stones in a plowed field
(v. 11).

In verse 12 Hosea again refers to the example of
Jacob. The historical thread, broken off at verse 6, is
resumed. Verses 12 and 13 contrast the hard lot of
Jacob in one of his experiences, namely, looking for a
wife, and that of Israel in her deliverance from Egypt
and entrance into the land of promise. Jacob served al-

most as a slave for some seven years for his wife without other remuneration. In contrast, Yahweh delivered Israel from Egypt by a prophet and gave the nation its rich heritage as a gift. After they were in the land Yahweh continued to provide and care for them. But what was the attitude and response of those so lovingly provided for and protected? Instead of gratitude to Yahweh for His blessings, Ephraim provoked Him to bitter anger by his disobedience and especially by his idolatry. Therefore, Ephraim's blood will be upon himself. He will bear the consequences of his own guilt (v. 14).

QUESTIONS FOR DISCUSSION

1. Chapter 11 of Hosea has been described as "one of the greatest chapters in the Bible." Do you agree? Why?

2. In chapter 11 Hosea paints the blackest picture possible of Israel's sin. Explain. Is this not the sin of every individual who rejects the love of Christ?

3. Explain how there is found or illustrated in chapter 11 the triumph of God's grace over man's sin. Does this in any way suggest that man is not accountable for his sins, or that he will not be punished for them (unless he by faith lays hold upon God's provision for the forgiveness of sin)?

4. Perhaps Jacob is most often remembered as a trickster or supplanter. Is there not another side to the man represented in the name "Israel" given him by God? How did Hosea make use of this better side of Jacob in his exhortations to the nation Israel? (See 12:2-6.)

C. The Ways of Death and Life (13:1–14:9)

1. Apostasy Results in Death (13:1-16)

This chapter serves well as a summary of much that has gone before: the early promise of Israel and Yahweh's tender care; Israel's forgetfulness and apostasy; the failure of kings and the stubborn stupidity of the people; and finally the inevitability of the coming judgment. This is indeed a dark chapter. It would be darker still if it were the final chapter, for it contains the prospect of unmitigated doom and destruction, the death knell for the nation.

a. Ephraim's Glory Turned to Shame (13:1-3)

Hosea describes the circumstances by which Ephraim (the tribe, not the nation Israel as he often uses that term) fell from the height of favor with God and man to the lowest depth. Jacob had blessed Ephraim above Manasseh (Gen. 48:18-20), and Ephraim stood high among the tribes during the period of the judges (Judg. 8:1-13; 12:1ff.). Also the first king of the ten tribes came from Ephraim (1 Kings 11:26ff.). Hosea points to Ephraim's exalted position in the words "when Ephraim spoke, men trembled" (v. 1), a time when Ephraim was "exalted in Israel." But his death warrant was signed when he allowed idolatry to enter his midst. "And now" (v. 2)–the Israel of Hosea's day is no better than was the Ephraim of old. The nation had accelerated its pace of sinning against Yahweh. From a perverted worship of Yahweh through the figure of the calf they had moved to worship the idol itself. Then they had increased their sin by making "molten images, idols skillfully made of their silver" and by expressing their devotion to the false deity by kissing the calves (or kissing the hand toward the calves). And because they worshiped what Jeremiah later described as "no gods" (Jer. 2:11), they themselves came to have no substance, no stability. Nothing plus nothing equals nothing! How fitting are the figures of verse 3, which illustrate the rapid passing away of Ephraim in the violent winds of Yahweh's judgment. Yahweh is eternal, but what Israel made and worshiped will be swept away along with the nation.

b. The Fate of Those Who Forget God (13:4-8)

Israel's conduct was the more tragic because Yahweh had proved Himself to be their protector and provider. He had been their God from Egypt (v. 4), and had repeatedly charged that they have no other god(s) than Himself. Israel's entire history revealed that Yahweh alone was their savior. There was none other to deliver them. The loving care of Yahweh was evident during Israel's wanderings in the wilderness, when hunger and thirst threatened to destroy them (v. 5).

But Yahweh's concern for Israel, and the resulting prosperity, failed to inspire the nation to a grateful response. Instead, it made them proud and arrogant, and they forgot their God (v. 6), the giver of their blessings (cf. Deut. 6:10-12; 8:7-20), and worshiped the creatures of their own hands (idols). It is only a short distance from forgetfulness to judgment. Therefore the God who has been their savior will now become their destroyer and devour them as do the wild beasts their prey.

c. Israel's Death Is Inevitable (13:9-16)

(1) Israel's kings helpless to save (13:9-13). The only help for Israel had been Yahweh; but she had forsaken and forgotten Him, therefore none was left. Israel's plight is hopeless. Who can help? The obvious answer is "No one." The idols cannot, for they are "no gods," the work of men's hands, impotent, and an impediment rather than a help. Hosea chides as he continues, "Where

now is your king, to save you?" (v. 10). When Israel first asked for a king, it was for defense against their enemies (cf. 1 Sam. 8:5), but their kings and princes had proved to be active in the nation's apostasy from Yahweh. This was particularly true in the northern kingdom of Israel where every king had been an idolator. From first to last not one had been a true worshiper of Yahweh, whose wrath was now upon king as well as people. Wicked rule followed wicked rule until Yahweh in His anger was about to destroy the institution of monarchy along with the nation that had identified itself with it. The iniquitous act of Israel in desiring a human king rather than Yahweh as king is sealed or "bound up" to be "kept in store" for the day of reckoning, just as legal records were stored for later reference. Thus Hosea seems to identify or link the destruction of the nation with the failure of the monarchy as an institution. Who can save Israel? No one, for they have rejected the Lord, and both idols and kings are utterly powerless to deliver. Furthermore, Yahweh, the only one who can help, has made His determination, "I will destroy you, O Israel" (v. 9a).

But Israel's death has not come without the chance for renewal and new life. She had numerous opportunities for repentance and renewal, but in her rebellion she had failed to act. In order to emphasize this failure Hosea compares the nation to an "unwise son" that is undergoing the pangs of birth but cannot be born because he refuses to "present himself at the mouth of the womb" (v. 13) at the time for delivery. Any such fetus which does not come forth from the womb, whatever the cause, faces certain death. God's prophets on numerous occasions had proclaimed to Israel the possibilities of a new life and had set forth the manner of entering into it, but the nation had stubbornly refused to enter. When an individual or a nation refuses life, the only alternative is death.

(2) Yahweh Himself will not save (13:14-16). From
the previous verses (9-13) it is evident that certain death
awaits the nation. None can save her except Yahweh
alone. But will He intervene? Shall He "ransom them from
the power of Sheol? Shall [He] redeem them from Death"
(v. 14a)? Or shall He allow death to have its way and
destroy His people? Does the verse contain a promise or
a threat? The Septuagint supports the former: "I shall
rend them out of the hand of death, and I shall redeem
them out of death." Paul, apparently following the spirit
(but not the exact words) of the Septuagint, took a
positive view of Hosea's words: "O death where is thy
victory? O death, where is thy sting?" (1 Cor. 15:55).
Nevertheless the words (v. 14a) contain a threat rather
than a promise. This view is supported by the context in
which verse 14a is situated (note the threat found in vv.
9-13 which precede, and in vv. 15-16 which follow). It is
also supported by the rendering, "Compassion is hid
from my eyes" (v. 14b). The prophet's point is clear.
There is a limit to the patience of God; He will no longer
show compassion to Israel. So the Lord will not ransom
them (Israel) from the power of Sheol. He will not redeem them from death. Instead He calls upon both to
do their worst against Israel: "O Death, where are your
plagues? O Sheol, where is your destruction?"

Verses 15 and 16 continue the thought of the doom
just announced by describing the certainty of Israel's
destruction as death and Sheol bring their worst against
the land. Though Israel has been a productive plant
flourishing in the water, "the wind of the Lord" (v. 15)
coming from the east—Assyria—will dry her up—plants,
springs, and fountains. Israel's wealth and treasure will
also be removed. And that is not all—human life will also
be at stake: "Their little ones shall be dashed in pieces,
and their pregnant women ripped open" (cf. Amos 1:13;
2 Kings 15:16). The picture of Israel's end is one of
disaster and destruction, the "ultimate doom," all be-

cause Samaria (for "Israel" here) "has rebelled against her God" (v. 16).

2. Repentance Results in Renewal and Life (14:1-9)

Hosea has used numerous forms of discourse in his prophetic utterances. In this last chapter he makes use of the form of a "liturgy of repentance" including the call to repentance (vv. 1-2a), the penitent's prayer (vv. 2b-3), and the divine response (vv. 4-8). The whole (including v. 9) provides an excellent conclusion and an appropriate summary of the prophet's message to Israel. If the reader of Hosea is puzzled as to how the prophet can turn so abruptly from the dark picture of judgment and destruction in chapter 13 to yet another call for sincere repentance on Israel's part, firm in his faith that God will forgive, let the reader be reminded of the prophet's graphic picture of Yahweh's love presented in chapter 11 (especially verses 8-9). Let him remind himself also that Hosea found in the example of Yahweh's undying love for Israel the dynamic of his own love for Gomer that compelled him to redeem her from the slave market of sin. Little wonder that Hosea is called the "Apostle John of the Old Testament"!

a. The Call to Repentance (14:1-2a)

Hosea's call for Israel to repent is simple but urgent: "Return" (Heb., *shub*) is the word characteristically used in the Old Testament to describe that turning which must accompany true repentance. Israel has traveled along a route leading further and further away from Yahweh; now she must return ("repent") and travel toward "your God." In view of Israel's tendency to run after other gods, she needed to be reminded constantly that Yahweh was her *only* legitimate God. Also, before true repentance or return to the Lord can occur, Israel must recognize that her stone of stumbling is her sin. Hence the prophet declares: "You have stumbled because of your iniquity." This Israel *must* acknowledge; so indeed must every sinner. Every Israelite was familiar with the command: "None shall appear before me empty-handed" (Exod. 23:15; cf. 34:20). But Hosea is categorically against the *sacrifice-only* approach to Yahweh (5:6; 6:6; 8:13). Therefore, when Israel repents (returns) and comes before Yahweh, instead of Canaanitish sacrifices and idol worship she will offer sincere words of confession and supplication—words indicative of heartfelt repentance (v. 2a).

b. The Penitent's Prayer (14:2b-3)

Hosea sees prayer as the means of repentant Israel's access to God. The prayer begins with the central problem—the sin upon which the nation has stumbled: "Take away all iniquity" (v. 2b). This petition for forgiveness is a confession that they are sinners and a recognition that Yahweh alone by His own actions can overcome their past failures. Israel is to further petition her God to receive the "good service" which Israel will now render Him, namely, confession of sin and vows of obedience. "And we will render the fruit of our lips" (RSV) is difficult. A literal rendering gives "And we will render calves our lips." The meaning seems to be that instead of offering sacrifices of calves, the sacrifice of lips will be offered, that is, words of confession, petition, thanksgiving, and praise (hence the Revised Standard Version rendering, "fruit of our lips").

A second element in this prayer of the penitent is a series of vows by which Israel is to declare her consecration to Yahweh. The two besetting sins of the nation were their trust for safety in foreign alliances and their allegiance to the fertility Baals, against both of which Hosea had brought repeated indictments. Repentant Israel vows to renounce both as the object of her trust and devotion and to rely upon Yahweh alone (v. 3a). The affirmation of Israel's trust, "In thee the orphan finds mercy" (v. 3b), supplies that element of confidence and praise needed and expected in this penitential prayer. Neither foreign alliances nor man-made idols can offer man that which he so desperately needs. Yahweh alone is able and willing to show loving-kindness and mercy.

c. The Divine Response (14:4-8)

In response to Israel's words of confession, consecration, and trust, Yahweh responds through the prophet that He stands ready in unqualified love to "heal their faithlessness" (v. 4). He loves them of His own free will, spontaneously and not because they deserve it. And, as they have sincerely repented, His "anger has turned from them."

In order to portray the renewal and life that results from sincere repentance, Hosea makes use of metaphors drawn from mother nature (vv. 5-8). Yahweh "will be as the dew to Israel." Hosea mentions "dew" earlier (6:4; 13:3) as a type of things transitory and passing; here it represents that which refreshes and renews life. Yahweh will be to His repentent people as the refreshing dew, reviving them as the abundant dew of Palestine revives vegetation withered by a burning sun. Then Israel, in the right relationship with Yahweh, will grow luxuriantly even "as the lily" and with "roots" as the cedars of "Lebanon" ("poplar," RSV). The entire picture is one of renewal, life, growth, beauty, and productivity—all of which are the results of repentance.

Hosea's "liturgy of repentance" closes with verse 8: "O Ephraim, what have I to do with idols?" Some translations put these words in Ephraim's mouth and read: "Ephraim shall say, what have I to do anymore with idols?" It is preferable to view the question as coming from Yahweh. It is true that Hosea once charged: "Ephraim is joined to idols" (4:17), but now with his turning to Yahweh the very name of Baalim will disappear from his lips and memory. The day of idolatry, then, is over and Yahweh will have nothing to do with idols for Ephraim has freed himself from them.

In the divine response to Israel's repentance, Yahweh has said, "I will heal" and "I will love" (v. 4), "I will be as the dew" (v. 5); the response concludes: "I am like an evergreen cypress, from me comes your fruit" (v. 8). The tree referred to could be any one of numerous coniferous trees. Identity is of small consequence, for the metaphor's main emphasis is on the tree's continuing greenness, undiminished by changing seasons. Since the cypress is nonfruitbearing, it is referred to not so much as a particular species or type, but as indicative of that which is constantly alive; indeed as the very source of life. In Yahweh alone, then, Israel will find true life. This is the marvelous message of Hosea in all of his oracles—a lasting legacy from the Lord for all who read his prophecy.

3. A Parting Admonition (14:9)

The final verse of the chapter is more than a conclusion to the material contained in the previous verses (1-8). It serves well as an epilogue or *finis* to the entire book, pointing to the moral emphasis which pervades and underlies its every page. It calls for serious reflection upon the teachings of the book and for all who read to lay them to heart. Such an exhortation is proper, for "the ways of the Lord are right"—that is, straight, undeviating, free from deceit—and real life is dependent upon knowing them. The righteous ("upright") obey what they learn and find the way to life, but "transgressors" ("rebels") stumble in disobedience and lose their way (cf. Ps. 1, especially v. 6). This stern reminder of the righteousness of Yahweh and of His demands on His people is most fitting. But it must not cause one to forsake the heights to which Hosea has lifted him. Man's hope and help reside in the God who, in spite of man's stubborn refusal to be upright and to walk in His ways, still loves and forgives. Aside from such a hope, there is no hope at all.

QUESTIONS FOR DISCUSSION

1. Do you see a similarity or relationship in the central idea or thought expressed in Hosea 13–14 and that expressed in Psalm 1 and in Christ's words in Matthew 7:13-14? Express this idea in a brief statement.

2. What is the dominant mood or note of the final chapter of Hosea? Is such an ending characteristic of the messages of the prophets? (Cf. Amos 9:11-15; Joel 3:16-21; Obad. 17-21; Mic. 7:18-20.)

3. In regard to the two choices Hosea placed before Israel in these chapters (13–14), which did Israel choose? Is every man faced with the same choice?

4. Hosea has been called "the prophet of God's love." As you look back over the entire book, point out several passages which magnify that love.

5. Make a list of lessons, teachings, or truths from the Book of Hosea which you think are particularly pertinent or relevant to your individual or to our national life.

6. What do you consider as the most notable contribution of the prophet Hosea?

BIBLIOGRAPHY

Brown, S. L., "The Book of Hosea," *Westminister Commentaries.* London: Methuen & Co., Ltd, 1932.

Calkins, Raymond, *The Modern Message of the Minor Prophets.* New York: Harper & Brothers, 1947.

Freeman, Hobart E., *An Introduction to the Old Testament Prophets.* Chicago: Moody Press, 1968.

Honeycutt, Roy L., "Hosea," *Broadman Bible Commentaries,* vol. 7. Nashville: Broadman Press, 1972.

Mauchline, John, "The Book of Hosea," *Interpreter's Bible,* vol. 6. Nashville: Abingdon Press, 1956.

Mays, James L., *Hosea.* Philadelphia: The Westminister Press, 1969.

Myers, Jacob M., "The Book of Hosea," *The Layman's Bible Commentary,* vol. 14. Richmond: John Knox Press, 1959.

Paterson, John, *The Goodly Fellowship of the Prophets.* New York: Charles Scribner's Sons, 1949.

Smith, George Adam, *The Book of the Twelve Prophets,* vol. 1. New York: Harper & Bros., 1896.

White, K. Owen, *Studies in Hosea.* Nashville: Convention Press, 1947.

Yates, Kyle M., *Preaching from the Prophets.* Nashville: Broadman Press, 1942.